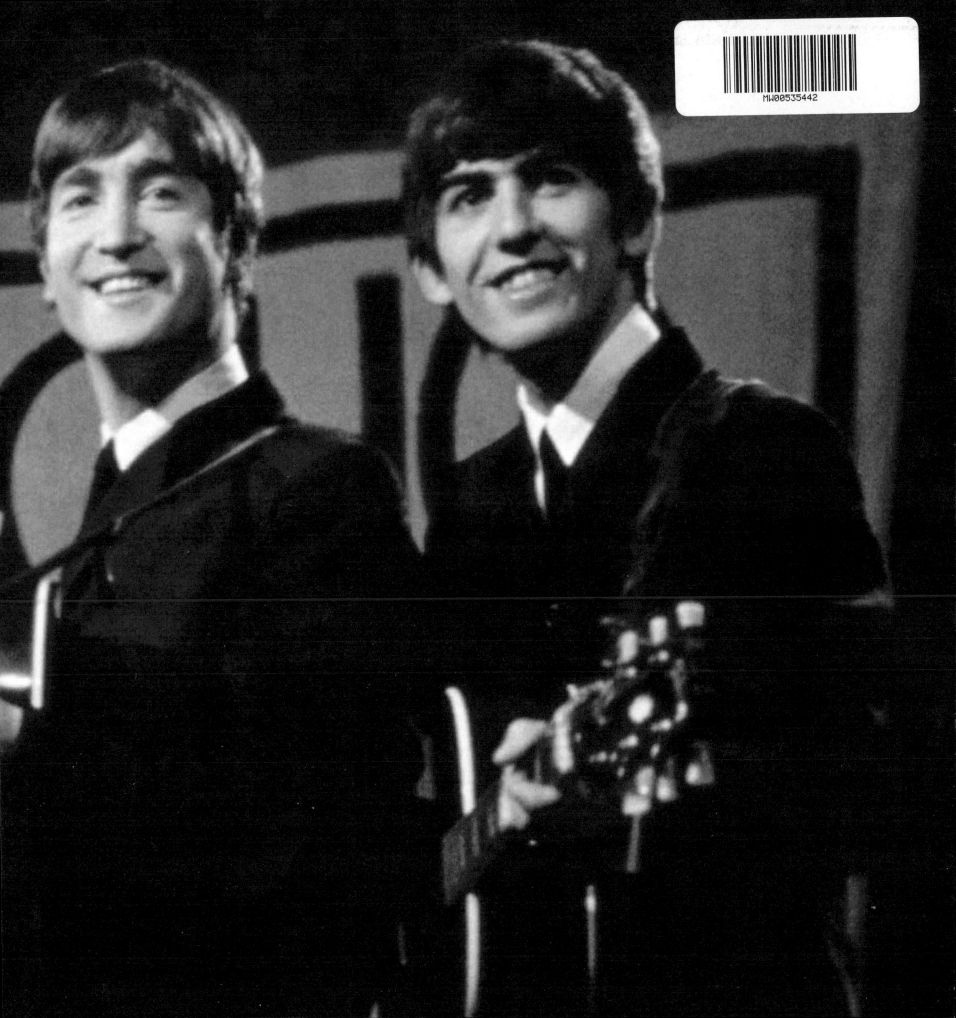

The Beatles
Uncut The Long Winding Road

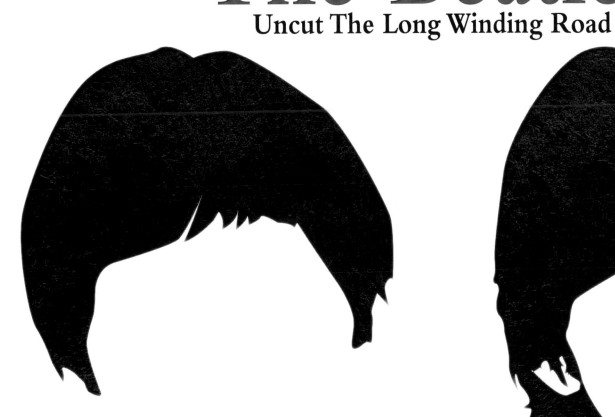

4 DVD BOOK SET COLLECTORS LIMITED EDITION
UNOFFICIAL AND UNAUTHORISED

First Published by FHE Ltd

CAT NO: BZB0263

Photography courtesy Pictorial Press, Wikimedia Commons, Getty Images unless indicated otherwise.

Made in EU.

ISBN: 9780993017025

Contents

CHAPTER ONE

Despite the fact that nearly 45 years have passed since The Beatles broke up, the quartet from Merseyside remain the yardstick by which success and popularity in non-classical music are measured. Any time a new act shows promise of rising above the usually short life at the top, they are dubbed potential new Beatles, but, of course, none have ever managed to reach the hallowed position of the Fab Four.

Perhaps The Beatles were fortunate in the era when they were active. Elvis Presley dominated the 1950s, and The Beatles did the same in the 1960s, but since then any act that claims to have similarly dominated a decade will certainly struggle to find unanimity among the experts, commentators and critics who make such judgements.

The Beatles arrived at the right time, just as Elvis had a few years earlier. Since then, no act has made such a massive international impression, and the likelihood of such an event ever happening again is remote. The Beatles remain the only group to ever create headlines all over the world. Not that it was all good news…

There are innumerable accounts of how the group progressed from obscurity to massive fame in early 1963, but that is not the subject of this book, which will endeavour to cast a critical eye on the dozen original albums released by the group from 1962's 'Please Please Me' to 1970's 'Let It Be'.

In 1960, The Beatles were just one of many groups playing enthusiastic versions of songs written by Chuck Berry and other mainly black American R&B stars. These include The Shirelles, a female vocal quartet from Passaic, New Jersey, or Little Richard, a piano-pounding rocker, who, many years later, was confirmed as self-confessedly gay.

There were exceptions to the skin colour preference – George Harrison's major idol in the early days was Carl Perkins, a country singer who had arrived at the holy grail of rock'n'roll via a diametrically opposite door from Chuck Berry but was similarly adored and admired by young British rockers.

When The Beatles recorded the 14 tracks that make up their first album 'Please Please Me', their repertoire included six cover songs, although it is probably true to say that few of these were widely known before The Beatles made them familiar.

'Anna (Go To Him)' introduced Arthur Alexander to UK audiences, and when The Rolling Stones recorded 'You Better Move On' early in their career, he must have felt that these white boys from England loved him to death.

'Chains' was another covered US hit by a black act largely unknown in Britain, although we now know that The Cookies frequently worked with Gerry Goffin & Carole King, the husband and wife team who wrote, arranged and produced the song. Two tracks on the 'Please Please Me' album were covers of songs recorded by The Shirelles. 'Baby It's You' was co-written by Burt Bacharach, and had been a US Top 10 hit at the start of 1962. Like both 'Anna' and 'Chains', the Beatles version featured John Lennon as lead vocalist. Over 30 years later, in 1995, a version of 'Baby It's You', recorded as part of a BBC session, was released as a single which made the UK Top 10.

'Boys', the other Shirelles song on 'Please Please Me', had been a B-side for the girl group and was selected as a showcase for lead vocals, by Beatles drummer Ringo Starr. This song was possibly known to a discerning few in Britain beforehand as it had been the B-side to The Shirelles' first US chart-topper, 'Will You Love Me Tomorrow', one of the greatest pop songs ever written.

Another cover was 'Twist And Shout', which became the final track recorded for this debut album by The Beatles, and was also the last track when the LP appeared in the shops. The song had been written under the alias of Medley/Russell by American songwriter/producer Bert Russell Berns, who had produced a version of the song by The Isley Brothers. The song became the family group's first US Top 20 hit. Much has been made of the fact that John Lennon's lead vocal betrayed the fact that he was exhausted after a long day in the recording studio, but this is arguably the best-loved track on the 'Please Please Me' album, bringing an extraordinary collection of music to a suitably climactic conclusion.

The sixth cover version on the album was 'A Taste Of Honey', a song written by Bobby Scott and Ric Marlow as the title music for a 1960 stage play, a 'kitchen sink' drama by English playwright Shelagh Delaney. The song had been recorded several times as an instrumental – including, in Britain, by The Victor Feldman Quartet and by Acker Bilk, whose version was a UK Top 20 hit in early 1963, and in the US by Martin Denny, whose version was a Top 50 hit. The first vocal version of the song was by US pop singer Lenny Welch, but the song's inclusion on the 'Please Please Me' LP made it suddenly familiar. It was the only cover version on the album with a lead vocal by Paul McCartney.

Later in their careers, The Beatles would make several albums entirely of original songs written by one or more members of the group, but for this first album, they were understandably less confident about their songwriting ability. George Martin, who produced virtually all the group's recorded output, may not have been convinced that at this early stage they were capable of a complete album of worthwhile material. Even so, both sides of the group's first two singles were songs written by John Lennon and Paul McCartney, although the LP sleeve of the 'Please Please Me' album curiously credits them to McCartney/Lennon.

A measure of just how uncertain Martin felt about his new clients was that for their first single, 'Love Me Do' and its flipside 'P.S. I Love You', the producer booked a session musician, Andy White, to play drums, as he was concerned that Ringo, who had joined the group only a few weeks earlier and reputedly had no previous studio experience, might not be ready for such a crucial debut recording. Thus, there are two versions of 'Love Me Do', with Lennon and McCartney sharing lead vocals, one with Ringo on the drums, and the other with White drumming and Ringo playing maracas. The 'Please Please Me' album includes the Andy White version – not that many listeners would know, or even care! Of rather more significance is John Lennon's harmonica, which provides a hint of R&B, as it had on 'Chains'. While it wasn't a huge hit when released in early October 1962, 'Love Me Do' is important as the first hit single by The Beatles, even though it only peaked near the foot of the Top 20. 'P.S. I Love You' is not particularly notable and has never been regarded as a masterpiece.

The quartet recorded a version of their second single, 'Please Please Me', during the 'Love Me Do' sessions, but George Martin was unhappy with the arrangement they had used on this John Lennon composition, and asked them to try a different approach. There can be no doubt that Martin was absolutely correct, and the song was transformed into an irresistible and soulful plea, which turned a promising group into domestic stars, topping the UK chart. 'Ask Me Why', the single's flipside, was also a Lennon song and like

'P.S. I Love You', displays little finesse. It has been generally accepted that, at the time, the group were still learning how to write songs.

Of the remaining four original songs on the album, two were acceptable, and one, 'I Saw Her Standing There', inspired. The latter was largely a McCartney composition, and just as 'Twist And Shout' was a perfect final track for the album, 'I Saw Her Standing There' was an excellent opener. 'Do You Want To Know A Secret?' and 'Misery' were both covered by other British artists, although they enjoyed contrasting fortunes. 'Do You Want To Know A Secret?' was written by Lennon and recorded by fellow Liverpudlian Billy J. Kramer. His single, which was produced by George Martin, topped the UK singles chart, which somewhat deflected criticism of the rather average version of the song by The Beatles on the 'Please Please Me' album and on George Harrison as lead vocalist. 'Misery' was apparently written for Helen Shapiro, with whom The Beatles had toured, but turned down by her producer. The song was actually covered by Kenny Lynch, a minor black British pop star of the early 1960s, whose version failed to chart. Once again,

this version was not too memorable by The Beatles and mercifully brief. 'There's A Place' is a much more optimistic Lennon song, and was covered without chart success by minor British pop group The Kestrels.

While it cannot be denied that 'Please Please Me' was a fabulously successful album, topping the UK chart for over six months, it may be as much remembered for its innovative use of cover versions of American R&B hits as for a rather patchy collection of original songs by Lennon & McCartney.

> " Our society is run by insane people for insane objectives. I think we're being run by maniacs for maniacal ends and I think I'm liable to be put away as insane for expressing that. That's what's insane about it. "
>
> John Lennon

CHAPTER TWO

By the spring of 1963, The Beatles were a phenomenon of British pop music, with a chart-topping debut album, a Number One single in 'Please Please Me', frequent radio and TV appearances and a sold out national tour. When they returned to Abbey Road studios with producer George Martin, they were able to spend a few hours longer on their second album. The final ten tracks of 'With The Beatles' – four tracks had already been released as singles – were recorded in a single 16-hour session at a cost of just £400. 'With The Beatles' was completed in a single day – the 15th of July 1963. This is in stark contrast to today's superstars, who can spend many months on recording an album at massive cost.

Even before they started work on 'With The Beatles', the group had released two more singles, 'From Me To You'/'Thank You Girl' and 'She Loves You'/'I'll Get You', both of which topped the UK chart. All four of these songs were written by Lennon & McCartney, and none of these tracks appeared on a Beatles album in Britain until some time later, as the general feeling at the time was that it was somehow cheating fans by including hit singles on new albums, even though both 'Love Me Do' and 'Please Please Me' had both appeared on the 'Please Please Me' album. This philosophy has, of course, changed substantially in the last 40 years, and it is difficult now to find new albums that do not feature previous hit singles.

When 'With The Beatles' was released in November 1963, it was inevitably successful, and once again included 14 songs, eight of which were group originals, while the remaining half a dozen were cover versions. George Martin had told the group that he wanted to base their debut album on songs in their stage set, as this would mean that time would not be wasted in learning material. 'With The Beatles' was recorded in a similar manner, although this time, the group had recorded three of the cover versions previously on the 1st of January 1962, when they had unsuccessfully auditioned for Decca Records.

Among the songs they performed for Decca were 'Please Mr. Postman', 'Money', and 'Till There Was You'. The first two were from an opposite source to the third. 'Please Mr. Postman' was the first and biggest hit by girl quintet The Marvelettes and was written, according to the sleeve of 'With The Beatles', by 'Dobbin-Garrett-Garman-Brianbert'. However, 'The Book Of Golden Discs' suggests it was written by 'B. Holland, R. Bateman and F. Gorman'. Internet encyclopaedia Wikipedia provides what seems the most feasible explanation. When The Marvelettes auditioned for Berry Gordy's Tamla/Motown label, group member Georgeanna Dobbins needed an original song for their audition and borrowed a blues song from her friend William Garrett, which she then rearranged for the group. Dobbins left the group after the audition, and Gordy hired 'Brianbert' – songwriters Brian Holland and Robert Bateman – to rework the song. Freddie Gorman, another of Holland's songwriting partners (before Holland became part of the Holland/Dozier/Holland team) was also involved in the final version.

'Please Mr. Postman' was the very first Motown record to reach the top of the US singles chart, and any doubt about its worth as a song must surely have disappeared when it was revived in 1975 by The Carpenters, who restored it to the US Number One position.

'Money', sometimes better known as 'Money (That's What I Want)', was the first Motown single to sell a million copies, pre-dating 'Please Mr. Postman', and was originally a US hit in 1960 for Barrett Strong. The song was written by Janie Bradford and Motown founder Berry Gordy Jr. and became a popular part of the repertoire of numerous British beat groups during the mid-1960s. Others who recorded it include The Rolling Stones and The Searchers. Both these Motown songs were obvious crowd-pleasers in the group's live shows, and both featured lead vocals by John Lennon.

In contrast, 'Till There Was You' was a show tune, with Paul McCartney singing lead. The song, written by Meredith Willson, came from a 1950s stage musical, 'The Music Man', and was a US Top 30 hit in 1959 for beauty queen turned ballad singer Anita Bryant. It has been mentioned more than once that McCartney's penchant for theatrical ballads – 'A Taste Of Honey' had been on 'Please Please Me' – provided a strong contrast to Lennon's Motown leanings, which were underlined by yet another Detroit classic 'You Really Got A Hold One Me'. The song had been a US Top 10 single at the start of 1963 for Smokey Robinson & The Miracles. The Beatles' version featured shared lead vocals between Lennon and Harrison, and it was George who sang lead on the other two cover versions. One was quite familiar, Chuck Berry's 'Roll Over Beethoven', and the other, 'Devil In Her Heart', was a little known item by obscure girl group The Donays, who were probably from Detroit. Their 1962 version of the song was not a US hit, and if The Beatles had not recorded it, the song would surely have been forgotten.

The remaining eight tracks on 'With The Beatles' were group originals, with the exception of 'Don't Bother Me'. The song was written by George Harrison, supposedly the first time he had written both lyrics and tune for a song. Not that it's much of a highlight on the album, as can also

be said of 'Roll Over Beethoven' and 'Devil In Your Heart', although the other cover versions seem to have better stood the test of time.

The other seven originals are all Lennon/McCartney compositions, and the standout song was the mellifluous 'All My Loving', written and sung by McCartney, released as a US single, and became a 1964 hit, along with 'I Saw Her Standing There', 'Do You Want To Know A Secret', 'Twist And Shout', 'There's A Place' and 'Roll Over Beethoven', none of which were released as UK singles. The US hit singles were in addition to and simultaneously with 'She Loves You', 'Please Please Me', 'From Me To You', 'Thank You Girl', 'Love Me Do' and 'P.S. I Love You'. When America discovered The Beatles, the audiences behaved in an unrestrained manner, purchasing every Beatles single available in massive quantities. Another non-LP track, 'From Me To You', was both written and sung by Lennon & McCartney and remained at Number One in the UK for five weeks, while its flipside, 'Thank You Girl', was another joint effort both compositionally and vocally, and Lennon's harmonica makes another appearance. 'She Loves You'/'I'll Get You', released in August 1963, four months after 'From Me To You', was very much cut from similar cloth as the latter single, both sides featuring vocals from both Lennon and McCartney, who had written both songs jointly. Perhaps, in retrospect, the most significant aspect of 'She Loves You' was the 'Yeah, yeah, yeah' chorus, which became a trademark of the early Beatles' output. This single topped the UK chart for six weeks in two visits, and sold over a million copies in the UK alone, a major achievement. These two singles, typify the wide-ranging appeal of The Beatles.

Reverting to 'With The Beatles', the Lennon-composed opener 'It Won't Be Long' boasts considerable energy, while 'All I've Got To Do', also written by Lennon, comes as rather an anti-climax. 'Little Child', on which Lennon & McCartney again collaborated on both songwriting and vocals, is pleasant, and the same could be said of 'Hold Me Tight', largely a McCartney effort. The remaining two Lennon & McCartney songs on the album have interesting connotations: 'I Wanna Be Your Man', written mainly be McCartney and sung here by Ringo Starr, was written for The Rolling Stones, whose manager, Andrew Loog Oldham, had previously worked as publicist for The Beatles. Oldham told McCartney that the Stones were having difficulty in finding appropriate songs to record, whereupon he was given 'I Wanna Be Your Man', which became the Stones' first UK Top 10 hit. 'Not A Second Time', written by Lennon, was noted by the music critic of 'The Times' for its concluding 'Aeolian cadence', which he likened to 'Song Of The Earth' by classical composer Gustav Mahler.

Finally, the atmospheric black and white sleeve photograph of the quartet by Robert Freeman has been much copied subsequently.

From a musical point of view, most of the tracks on 'With The Beatles' have, in all honesty, not stood the test of time as well as many of the group's other original works.

> " One of my biggest thrills for me still is sitting down with a guitar or a piano and just out of nowhere trying to make a song happen. "
>
> Paul McCartney

> " I like Beethoven, especially the poems. "
>
> Ringo Starr

CHAPTER THREE

November 1963 was significant in world terms because that was the month when President John F. Kennedy was assassinated. This did have an effect on the music business in that American record buyers seemingly lost interest in new music. The greatest example of this was that Phil Spector spent most of the summer of 1963 recording what many feel is the greatest Christmas album ever made, 'A Christmas Gift For You'. The album featured acts signed to his label, including The Crystals, The Ronettes, Bob B. Soxx & The Blue Jeans, and Darlene Love, performing seasonal songs like 'Winter Wonderland', White Christmas' and 'Frosty The Snowman'. It is often regarded as Spector's greatest achievement, yet the American public were simply not interested, and seemed to have immersed themselves in mourning the death of their President.

It may not have been any kind of coincidence that Capitol Records, the US label to which The Beatles were signed, decided they were prepared to release 'I Want To Hold Your Hand'. After failing to release 'Love Me Do', 'Please Please Me'. 'From Me To You' and 'She Loves You', which had all been UK hit singles, they released the new Beatles single in Britain just before Christmas 1963. The group made their US television debut on the Ed Sullivan Show on the 18th of January 1964, after which America capitulated to the Merseybeat sound. Almost immediately after the Sullivan

show, the young record buyers of America forgot their grief over Kennedy's death as they found a smile at those Beatle heads shaking to 'Yeah, yeah yeah!' Before long, The Beatles had established a US chart domination which is unlikely to ever be equalled. In the first six months of 1964, no less than 19 Beatles singles reached the US Top 100.

Meanwhile, the group had started work on their first movie. Shooting began for 'A Hard Day's Night' in early March and ended in late April. The black and white film's title came from a chance remark made by Ringo Starr, and predictably, it was a massive success. The movie was a kind of film vérité of the group's hectic life, and also starred Wilfred Brambell (best known for his unforgettable portrayal of the father in the 'Steptoe And Son' TV series) playing Paul McCartney's grandfather, and Victor Spinetti.

The soundtrack album contained seven songs featured in the movie and seven new songs and was the first Beatles album on which Lennon & McCartney wrote all the songs. Included were two chart-topping singles, 'Can't Buy Me Love' (featured in the film)/'You Can't Do That' (on the LP, but not in the movie) released in March 1964, and 'A Hard Day's Night' (title track of LP and film)/'Things We Said Today' (also LP but not movie) in July. All four songs captured The Beatles at their best; also true of the other ten tracks on the album. McCartney was the main writer of 'Can't Buy Me Love' and 'Things We Said Today', while Lennon wrote the title song, one of the group's most memorable tracks, and the less impressive 'You Can't Do That'.

Less than two months before the LP was released, the 'Long Tall Sally' EP appeared. Three of the four tracks were covers of American rock'n'roll classics, while the fourth was a Beatle version of 'I Call Your Name', a song John Lennon had given to stablemate Billy J. Kramer. Lennon also sang lead on 'Slow Down', a Larry

Williams classic from 1958, while McCartney was at the microphone for 'Long Tall Sally', the Little Richard/Pat Boone 1956 hit. George Harrison didn't get a lead vocal at all, as the fourth track, a cover of the 1957 Carl Perkins hit 'Matchbox', featured Ringo.

Harrison's admiration for Perkins was such that at one time, in Hamburg, he supposedly called himself Carl Harrison, and prior to their breakthrough, the group had recorded such Perkins-related songs as 'Sure To fall (In Love With You)', 'Lend Me Your Comb' and 'Everybody's Trying To Be My Baby', the last of which would appear later in 1964 on the 'Beatles For Sale' album.

The 'Long Tall Sally' EP was widely regarded as good, but it was soon pushed into the shadows by 'A Hard Day's Night', arguably somewhat of an improvement on 'With The Beatles'. Of the other songs featured in the film, the best two are Lennon's lively 'I Should Have Known Better', which still retains its energetic appeal and was also a UK Top 40 hit for The Naturals, a fairly obscure combo from Harlow in Essex, and McCartney's dreamy 'And I Love Her', reputedly inspired by his girlfriend of the time, Jane Asher. A few years ago, it was estimated that there were over 370 cover versions of this song. The Beatles original was released as a US single, peaking just outside the Top 10 in mid-1964, while a cover by soul singer 'Little' Esther Phillips peaked just outside the US Top 50 in 1965.

Lennon wrote 'I Fell' and 'Tell Me Why', on both of which he duetted to good effect with McCartney, and 'I'm Happy Just To Dance With You' for George Harrison to sing. Lennon also wrote the lion's share of the non-movie material, in particular 'I'll Cry Instead', which was written for the film, but ultimately rejected by director Richard Lester, although Joe Cocker recorded a cover version, and 'Any Time At All', on which Lennon sounds wired, although neither 'When I Get Home' nor 'I'll Be Back' are likely to figure among the favourite Beatles songs of too many listeners.

While the entire 'A Hard Day's Night' album lasts only a few seconds over half an hour from start to finish, the speed at which it was prepared must have contributed to its lack of polish. Not that record buyers were concerned, as some years ago, the album was estimated to have sold over four million copies.

The first half of 1964 must have been the most hectic period of the group's existence. Apart from conquering America in a manner which will surely never be equalled, they had made their first film, had met world heavyweight boxing champion Cassius Clay (aka Muhammad Ali), and British Prime Minister Harold Wilson, had won three Ivor Novello Awards, presented by the Duke Of Edinburgh, dominated the Australian singles chart with the top five singles in one week, John Lennon had published his first book of quirky poetry, 'In His Own Write', and they had made their own TV special, 'Around The Beatles', directed by Jack Good.

Much of the footage included on the DVDs that form the visual part of this package comes from this period, including excerpts from 'A Hard Day's Night', 'Around The Beatles' and the Ed Sullivan Show. Fortunately, by the time 'Beatles For Sale' was released at the end of 1964, the hectic pace of making movies, recording new material and touring was something with which the group had come to terms.

CHAPTER FOUR

A personal opinion is that 'Beatles For Sale' is the best Beatles album from the period when they were still performing live concerts. Their last major show was in Candlestick Park, San Francisco on 29th August 1965. After that, they could afford the luxury of spending longer on songwriting and recording, but some have said that when the urgency was taken from The Beatles schedule, they became self-indulgent and sloppy, and it is hard to deny that the group's music changed when the frantic touring ended.

With 'Beatles For Sale', the group reverted to the tried and tested formula from their first two albums, mixing eight original songs with half a dozen favourite cover versions; but this time four of the cover versions were familiar, perhaps because those first two albums had reminded the record-buying public that there had been a golden age of rock'n'roll in the 1950s and that rockers like Buddy Holly, Chuck Berry and Carl Perkins were still around and capable of great music. While songs by Berry and Perkins had previously appeared on Beatle records, this was the first time that Buddy Holly's huge influence on the group had been openly acknowledged. After all, they had chosen their name, borrowed from the insect world, in polite homage to Holly's group, The Crickets. Holly's ability to not only write his great songs but also to sing them and to play lead guitar made him a role model for innumerable aspiring young British rock'n'roll fans and members of beat groups. 'Words Of Love' was the first Holly-connected song officially released

by The Beatles, although they had also recorded 'Crying, Waiting, Hoping' for a BBC session and 'Reminiscing' for a lo-fi album at the Star Club in Hamburg. Perhaps it was only reasonable that they should formally record a Buddy Holly song, especially as they had recorded so many songs associated with Carl Perkins, who few would rate as highly as Holly. Many years later, Paul McCartney acquired the music publishing rights to many of Holly's songs, no doubt on the basis that he still admired them, and also because he felt they were a very worthwhile investment. 'Words Of Love', written by Holly, appeared on his eponymous album released in the US in April 1958, one of only two albums featuring Holly which were released during his lifetime – the other one was 'The 'Chirping' Crickets' – and this great song was treated with appropriate respect by The Beatles, with Lennon and McCartney sharing lead vocals. Of the two Carl Perkins songs on the album, 'Honey Don't' was sung by Ringo and had appeared on the flip side of 'Blue Suede Shoes'. It was the biggest hit Perkins ever achieved, a reasonable attempt, considering that Ringo was a better drummer than vocalist. The less familiar 'Everybody's Trying To Be My Baby' was sung by the group's biggest Perkins fan at the time, George Harrison, with a rockabilly guitar solo well observed.

The Chuck Berry cover version is 'Rock And Roll Music', one of Berry's most anthemic compositions, and one that was a great favourite among British beat groups in the 1960s. On 'Beatles For Sale', Lennon sang it; apparently, he also played piano, sharing that job with McCartney and producer George Martin. Another cover was of the standard 'Kansas City', written by the American songwriting and production team of Jerry Leiber & Mike Stoller, and performed by Paul. It was, seemingly, a tribute to Little Richard, as the song is turned into a medley with another song, made famous by Richard Penniman, 'Hey, Hey, Hey, Hey'. Making up the half dozen cover versions was 'Mr.

Moonlight', a song that would have remained extremely obscure had it not been recorded by The Beatles. The original recording of the song, written by Roy Lee Johson, was by US R&B group Dr. Feelgood & The Interns, the leader of which was Piano Red (real name William Perryman), who accumulated five US R&B hits in 1950/51. John Lennon screams the lyrics of the song, which also appeared on the Star Club album referred to above. The American Dr. Feelgood has no connection other than in name with the 1970s R&B band from Southend, featuring vocalist Lee Brilleaux and guitarist Wilko Johnson.

A week before 'Beatles For Sale' was released in early December, a new Beatles single topped the charts on both sides of the Atlantic. 'I Feel Fine', written by Lennon, featured lead vocals by him with some assistance from McCartney and provided Ringo Starr, who had just undergone painful dental surgery, with the chance to tell journalists who enquired after his health, 'I feel fine'. McCartney wrote the B-side of the 45, 'She's A Woman', and also sang lead. The single deservedly became the group's fifth consecutive million-selling single, and was a perfect way to remind punters – as if they needed reminding – of the new LP.

Of the eight Lennon/McCartney songs included, three are arguably among the best tracks The Beatles ever recorded, and all were considered for release as singles until John Lennon came up with 'I Feel Fine'. The opening 'No Reply', a John Lennon song on which he sang lead, remains an excellent track, and surely could have been a hit single had it been released in this format, while 'I'm A Loser', another Lennon song on which he was also lead vocalist, was released in the US as the lead track on an EP titled '4 By The Beatles'. It was accompanied by three cover versions, 'Honey Don't', 'Everybody's Trying To Be My Baby' and 'Mr. Moonlight'. Although the 'Beatles '65' album included all

four songs and had been released a few weeks before and topped the US chart, '4 By The Beatles' remained in the US chart for five weeks, peaking not far outside the Top 50.

'Baby's In Black', a Lennon/McCartney collaboration as both songwriters and vocalists, seems to be one of the lesser tracks on 'Beatles For Sale', although McCartney's 'I'll Follow The Sun' is personally preferable. The next Beatles original was arguably the best track on the entire album. 'Eight Days A Week', with its innovative fade-in introduction was released as a single in the USA, appropriately topped the 'Billboard' chart, and was certified gold for a million sales. The song was another magic Lennon/McCartney moment and was jointly written and sung. The three other Lennon/McCartney compositions do not match up to the three regarded as potential singles. 'Every Little Thing' with McCartney singing lead was the subject of a cover version by progressive rock group Yes on their eponymous 1969 debut album, but Lennon's country-tinged 'I Don't Want To Spoil The Party' still sounds worthwhile, while McCartney's 'What You're Doing' sounds more routine and disposable. 'Beatles For Sale' still strikes a chord today, and if anyone is searching for the best Beatles album before everything became too frantic and silly, this is the one.

> "There are only four people who knew what the Beatles were about anyway."
>
> Paul McCartney

CHAPTER FIVE

The first new Beatles single of 1965 was 'Ticket To Ride'/'Yes It Is', both of which were written by John Lennon, whose output at this time was prolific. 'Ticket To Ride' became the group's fifth consecutive single to enter the UK chart at Number One, also topping the US chart. 'Yes It Is', which has an intriguing quality about it, also separately reached the Top 50 of the US chart. The major event of 1965 was the second Beatles movie 'Help!'. After the massive success of 'A Hard Day's Night', United Artists, the company that financed both films, allowed 'Help!' to be made in colour. Richard Lester was again hired to direct. Lester was highly acceptable to The Beatles due to his work with The Goons, including the wonderfully ludicrous 'The Running, Jumping And Standing Still Film', a short movie in which nothing really happened, but which strongly appealed to those with an absurdist sense of humour.

'Help!' was originally rumoured to be titled 'Eight Arms To Hold You', and filming took place in both the Austrian Alps and in The Bahamas as well as around Stonehenge, which certainly gave the film a more expensive look than its predecessor. Among the actors helping out were Leo McKern, Eleanor Bron, Roy Kinnear and Victor Spinetti again. The plot is somewhat unlikely, about a ring on Ringo's finger, but the main point of interest was the music.

The seven songs featured in the film were arguably superior to those in 'A Hard Day's Night'.

'Ticket To Ride', which had already topped the charts on both sides of the Atlantic, was included in 'Help!' in the same way as another established Number One, 'Can't Buy Me Love', had been used in 'A Hard Day's Night'. John Lennon's inspired title song, which remains one of the best-loved Beatles songs, was released as a single a couple of weeks before the album appeared, and unsurprisingly, it immediately reached Number One in both Britain and America. For once, the single's flipside failed to make the US chart separately. This was the raucous McCartney rocker, 'I'm Down', which sounds a little strained vocally and may rarely, if ever, have been played live.

'The Night Before' was both written and sung by Paul McCartney, as was 'Another Girl', and both are melodic and easily memorable, while John Lennon's 'You've Got To Hide Your Love Away' and 'You're Going to Lose That Girl' continued his run of strong songs. British folk group The Silkie, whose version was produced by John and Paul, had a UK Top 30 hit with a cover of 'You've Got To Hide Your Love Away'. The reason why these superstars were working with a virtually unknown folk combo was probably that the band members of The Silkie, who were attending Hull University, were also being looked after by Beatles manager Brian Epstein. The other original song in the 'Help!' movie was 'I Need You' written by George Harrison, arguably the least memorable song in the film, although it is far from being a disaster.

Among the seven songs on the album but not in the movie is one that is often cited as the most covered and therefore best-selling Beatles song of all, 'Yesterday'. It also includes at least two of what may be among the most forgettable Beatles songs in George Harrison's 'You Like Me Too

Much', and Paul McCartney's 'Tell Me What You See'. Fortunately, McCartney largely redeems himself with the impressive 'I've Just Seen A Face', which was covered by American bluegrass group The Dillards, who demonstrated that the best pop songs are capable of being interpreted in many other musical genres.

Two cover versions were included on the album, one primarily to ensure that Ringo's vocal prowess was highlighted, as he had not been given the opportunity to sing lead on any of the songs in the movie. 'Act Naturally' had been the first of over 20 US Country chart-toppers for Buck Owens, one of the biggest country stars of the 1960s, although, curiously, the song had been part-written by Johnny Russell, who himself became a country star but only eight years after this success as a songwriter.

Ringo was always partial to country music, as was evidenced by one of his early solo albums, 'Beaucoups Of Blues', which was recorded in Nashville, and his straightforward version of 'Act Naturally' surely gave Johnny Russell's bank balance a boost, especially as the version by The Beatles was a US Top 50 hit single when it was released as the flipside of 'Yesterday'. The other 'outside' song was another Larry Williams rock classic, 'Dizzy Miss Lizzy', with lead vocal by John Lennon, who had also been lead vocalist on another Larry Williams song, 'Slow Down', on the 'Long Tall Sally' EP in 1964.

Which leaves 'Yesterday'. Both this McCartney composition and 'Act Naturally' were omitted from the US version of the Help!' album, and were released together as a single, which sold over a million copies in ten days. The story goes that Paul McCartney, who wrote the song, was unable to think of an appropriate title when he first wrote the song. For some time he referred to it as 'scrambled eggs', as the latter words have the correct number of syllables for the

musical phrase he had written. Fortunately, he came up with the title of 'Yesterday', and more than 2,500 artists have covered this wistful love song.

McCartney is the only Beatle on the recording, singing and playing guitar backed by a string quartet. The recording topped the charts in Belgium, Finland, Hong Kong and Norway, and was finally released as a single in the UK in 1976, when 23 Beatles singles were issued simultaneously, all the others having been previously released as singles in the UK.

This is perhaps an appropriate place to document the marital status of the four Beatles when they were most famous pop stars in the world. The first Beatle to marry had been John Lennon, who had married his pregnant girl friend Cynthia Powell on the 23rd of August 1962. Ringo Starr was next, marrying his long-time girlfriend, Maureen Cox, on the 11th of February 1965. Paul McCartney's steady girlfriend at the time was Jane Asher, the daughter of a Harley Street doctor. Jane's brother, Peter Asher, was one half of Peter & Gordon, who, perhaps as a result, were the fortunate recipients of Lennon/McCartney songs like their chart-topping debut, 'A World Without Love' and their Top 10 follow-up, 'Nobody I Know'. McCartney and Jane Asher announced their engagement at Christmas 1967, but a few months later, called it off. George Harrison, meanwhile, had met model Pattie Boyd on the set of 'A Hard Day's Night', and they were married on 21st January 1966.

> " We're more popular than Jesus.
>
> John Lennon

CHAPTER SIX

Another Number One Beatles single, 'Day Tripper'/'We Can Work It Out', was released at the start of December 1965, bringing to an end a fantastically successful year.

Apart from another string of massively-selling singles and albums, the group won two Grammy Awards and were each awarded the MBE in the Queen's Birthday Honours List, which resulted in a number of holders of the decoration returning it in disgust. The group later claimed that they had smoked marijuana in the Buckingham Palace toilets. John Lennon's second book of drawings and poetry, 'A Spaniard In The Works', was published, and the quartet met Elvis Presley for the first and only time when they visited his mansion in Bel Air. Reportedly they all sang together the Lennon & McCartney song 'You're My World', which had been a UK hit for Cilla Black. It seems unlikely that anyone had the presence of mind to have taped this summit meeting, or we would surely have seen at least a bootleg, if not a legal release of such a potentially huge collaboration. Lennon asked why he had stopped making rock'n'roll records, and Elvis replied that his film commitments left him very little time for anything else. This came a few days after the group's appearance at Shea Stadium in New York in front of a crowd of over 55,000 screaming fans.

'Day Tripper' was largely a Lennon composition, and he shared lead vocals with McCartney, who wrote and sang 'We Can Work It Out'. Interestingly, two American soul stars recorded cover versions, Otis Redding of 'Day Tripper' and Stevie Wonder of 'We Can Work It Out'. Wonder scored a US Top 20 hit in 1971, but Redding's super-funky cover remained an album track. Just before Christmas 1965, the sixth Beatles album, 'Rubber Soul', was released. Neither 'Day Tripper' nor 'We Can Work It Out' was included on the album, which did include several hit singles, although none were by The Beatles.

The opening track, 'Drive My Car', was written and sung by John & Paul, and was a minor US hit in 1966 for Bob Kuban & The In-Men. Nearly a decade later, it became a US hit in 1975 for New York disco act Gary Toms Empire, and in 1981 was included as part of the million-selling US chart-topping 'Stars On 45' medley.

However, the original version on 'Rubber Soul' remains the greatest. The next track, the somewhat lyrically curious 'Norwegian Wood (This Bird Has Flown)', written and sung by Lennon, was never a hit single for anyone, although it was the subject of numerous cover versions, including one by surf stars Jan & Dean, and various orchestral versions. The plot of this song is apparently about Lennon having an affair with someone and writing a song about the situation to disguise the facts to allay his wife's suspicions. The track is superbly recorded, but careful attention to the lyrics provides a considerable contrast – Lennon at his most satirical, vitriolic, and cruel.

McCartney's 'You Won't See Me' is pleasant but hardly exceptional, and the song was a US Top 10 hit for Canadian star Anne Murray in 1974. Later that year, her cover version of 'Day Tripper' also made the US chart. 'Nowhere Man' is another Lennon composition, and the perceived wisdom is that he was in the garden of his home trying to write a song, without success – until he portrayed himself as a nowhere man, doing nothing and going nowhere. The song was covered by an exceedingly obscure group known as Three Good Reasons, whose cover version briefly made the UK Top 50 more than 40 years ago, although hardly anything is known about the group. Were they American girls, as a very faint memory suggests, or were they a British male trio, as a book about beat groups maintains? Proof is needed…

'Think For Yourself' was written by George Harrison, who also sang lead, but this may be the first song on 'Rubber Soul' which didn't attract a cover version, although a song of this title was recorded by The Temptations in 1977, and by a combo known as D.R.I. (an abbreviation apparently of Dirty Rotten Imbeciles, a late 1980s Texas metal/punk band), but neither seems too likely to have covered the original.

Then comes 'The Word', a Lennon/McCartney song on which the former sings the verse, while the latter joins him for the chorus with George Harrison, and which was also covered as part of a medley on the first American 'Stars On 45' album 'Stars On Long Play'.

The final track on side one of the LP is 'Michelle', which is McCartney at his most sentimental, and includes a passage which he sings in French. The track was described in an otherwise generally favourable book on the group as 'flatulent and sugary', and it is light years away from the music that made them famous. British group The Overlanders covered the song; their version topped the UK singles chart for a week, while another British cover, by David & Jonathan (aka songwriters Roger Cook & Roger Greenaway) also made the UK and US Top 20s. 'Michelle' is one of the most covered Beatle songs, with well over 600 versions by 1985.

The second side of 'Rubber Soul' again includes a number of songs to be covered by other artists, although 'What Goes On', written originally by Lennon but with additions by McCartney and lead-singing Ringo Starr was not one of

them. By contrast, 'Girl', like 'Michelle', became a UK Top 20 hit for two other acts, St. Louis Union, a Manchester group, and Truth, a British beat group whose members included chief Groundhog Tony McPhee. Had The Beatles released 'Girl' as a single, it would surely have topped the charts on both sides of the Atlantic, but it wasn't, allowing a couple of minor groups a few minutes of fame. America was less interested – Jay & The Americans included a song titled 'Girl' on their 1966 'Greatest Hits' album, but it may have been a different song.

'I'm Looking Through You' is a McCartney song with more edge than usual, as it is supposedly his reflection on the end of his engagement to Jane Asher, which occurred because Ms. Asher decided to accept an offer to join the Bristol Old Vic Theatre company, which involved living in that part of the country. No one seems to have covered it. However, Lennon's 'In My Life' became the title track of a 1967 Judy Collins album, and was also covered by an army of other acts including Jose Feliciano and Rod Stewart. It's a reflective song, and perhaps displays another side of a man who sometimes seemed to act before thinking about the consequences, one reason why he was so admired. The final three tracks on the album are considered OK, if not exceptional. 'Wait' is a genuine Lennon/McCartney collaboration, on which Lennon sings lead, but the overriding impression 40 years later is that whoever is playing the tambourine should be less enthusiastic.

Harrison's 'If I Needed Someone', on which he sings lead, is OK, if slightly controversial. The Hollies, whose track record of UK hit singles in the 1960s was second to none, recorded a cover that made the UK Top 30, but was stopped in its tracks when George publicly expressed his distaste for their version. It is difficult to describe why he might have felt so upset, as this is unlikely to figure in the list of favourite tracks of many Beatles' fans and without

the controversy would probably have been forgotten by all but diehard fans. Finally, Lennon's 'Run For Your Life' was similarly controversial because its writer himself criticised the song as having been done in too much of a hurry – 'knocked off ' as he put it – to be worth very much, although, in all honesty, it really isn't that bad. This album shows The Beatles in transition, having made the decision to give up the punishing touring schedule, which by this time had lasted for well over five years.

The idea was to spend more time on songwriting and recording, without the need to hurry because they were expected somewhere else. Their final live concert took place on 29th August 1966, at Candlestick Park, San Francisco, but until then, they would be as busy as ever, with another album to complete. The first half of 1966 saw major controversy explode after an interview with John Lennon in the 'Evening Standard', during which he told Maureen Cleave: 'Christianity will go. It will vanish and shrink. I needn't argue about that, I'm right and I'll be proved right'. His next sentence was the one that he must have subsequently regretted saying: 'We're more popular than Jesus. I don't know which will go first, rock'n'roll or Christianity. Jesus was all right, but his disciples were thick and ordinary'.

John Lennon could always be relied upon to make headlines, but later in 1966, he would probably have been more than happy to eat those words.

CHAPTER SEVEN

June 1966 saw The Beatles briefly appear to lose their vice-like grip on the UK chart. They released a new single, 'Paperback Writer'/'Rain', which did not enter the chart at Number One, just failing to unseat Frank Sinatra's 'Strangers In The Night' in its first week in the chart, and stopping at Number Two, although a week later it was at the top. The A-side was a McCartney composition and lead vocal, which seems routine with the benefit of 40 years of familiarity, while 'Rain', which was written and sung by Lennon and has been described as 'psychedelic' is more interesting because of its weirdness, with an early example of a passage played backwards (by simply playing a tape from end to beginning, rather than the conventional start to finish. The results are as often quite intriguing as they are meaningless and unlistenable). The single's comparative failure in the UK, although it could hardly be termed a disaster, was the start of a very disturbing few months when all kinds of things seemed to go wrong.

Probably the first thing, although it was barely noticed on this side of the Atlantic, was an album released in the US titled 'Yesterday And Today'. For reasons relating to American copyright law, various tracks from both 'Help!' and 'Rubber Soul' had been omitted from the US releases of those albums, and with the addition of three tracks from the forthcoming 'Revolver' album and both sides of the 'Day Tripper'/'We Can Work It Out' single, an album was assembled which topped the US chart for three weeks. Conveniently, one of the tracks omitted from the American 'Help!' album was 'Yesterday', which, with 'Act Naturally', had been released as a single, and gave the 'Yesterday And Today' album half its title.

There was considerable controversy surrounding the album sleeve, which portrayed the group wearing butcher's smocks and surrounded by lumps of meat and dismembered dolls. Weird, but due to what has become known as 'the butcher sleeve', which was fairly quickly withdrawn and replaced by a much blander photograph of the band, the album became immensely collectable, although musically, there was nothing actually rare about it.

The three 'Revolver' tracks on 'Yesterday And Today' were 'I'm Only Sleeping', 'Doctor Robert', and 'She Said She Said'. The three were among the least prominent tracks on the album, although the latter two had subtexts concerning drugs. In fact, one commentator has suggested that even Lennon's 'I'm Only Sleeping', with its backwards guitars, was also symptomatic of his interest in the causes and effects of psychedelic substances. 'Doctor Robert', another song largely written by Lennon, is reputedly the name given to a New York physician who numbered many musicians among his clientele, as he was not averse to prescribing drugs (amphetamines) to keep them awake at times when they should have been asleep. 'She Said She Said', again written largely by Lennon, is said to concern his second LSD trip in Los Angeles, when he was with movie star Peter Fonda. All three tracks are engaging, if not especially commercial.

George Harrison has three tracks on 'Revolver', including the opener 'Taxman', which has often been cited as expressing his reputed annoyance at the amount of income tax he was having to pay as a Beatle. The Prime Ministers of the era, Wilson and Heath (Harold and Edward, respectively) are name-checked. The track is probably Harrison's best composition up to this point, although the lyrical griping seems a bit unnecessary – who would refuse the chance to make as much money as a Beatle, even if it came with a huge tax burden? The second Harrison track, 'Love You Too', is an Indian piece on which he both sings and plays sitar although probably not both at once, while the main backing instrument is a tabla (an Indian drum), played by Anil Bhagwar. While this is better (shorter) than some of George's later Indian pieces, some are still averse to the inclusion.

The third and last Harrison track, 'I Want To Tell You', would be OK (but not much more) if McCartney's utterly inappropriate (and almost insultingly amateurish) piano had been excluded. It's as if McCartney bore a gigantic grudge against his colleague, but perhaps the extremely dodgy piano is the only reason anyone remembers the track at all.

July was the worst month of 1966 for The Beatles. After a brief Japanese tour at the end of June, they flew to Manila in The Philippines, at the time controlled by dictator Ferdinand Marcos. Many may be more familiar with the name of his wife, Imelda, who was the subject of considerable international publicity when it became clear that she owned an incredible number of shoes. The erstwhile Miss Manila was known as the 'Steel Butterfly'. In 1986, when the Marcos regime was overthrown, it was discovered that she had literally thousands of pairs of very expensive shoes, while the vast majority of Filipino people were living in extreme poverty.

When The Beatles arrived at Manila airport, a huge crowd was waiting for them, and the military police boarded the plane and arrested the group. George Harrison was quoted as saying: 'These gorillas, huge guys, took us off the plane and confiscated our luggage'. They were put on a boat in Manila harbour and later were guests on a private yacht, where a rich local showed them off to his friends.

They were allowed to go to their hotel at four a.m. Unfortunately, Imelda Marcos had arranged a massive lunch for later that day, which the exhausted group didn't attend, as they were also due to play two shows that same day. Beatles manager Brian Epstein maintained that he knew nothing about the lunch, and although the shows apparently went well, the word was passed around that the group had insulted Mrs. Marcos, and from then until the group's flight out of Manila the next afternoon, they were forced to manage without security, and some of the party were manhandled. Harrison said: 'The only way I'd ever return to The Philippines would be to drop an atom bomb on it', which, for the most obviously pacifist Beatle, was an indication of the extreme conditions the group endured. Three weeks later, an American magazine published Lennon's interview with Maureen Cleave, and there was an outburst of bonfires of Beatles records in Alabama and other Bible belt states. The whole thing was getting completely out of hand, largely because Lennon's remarks were being taken out of context, and finally, on the 11th of August at a press conference in Chicago, Lennon publicly apologized, averting another crisis.

This allowed everyone to concentrate on 'Revolver', which had just been released and in the UK had been accompanied on the same day by a single of two of the most notable tracks on the album, although their appeal was for opposite reasons.

The initial idea for 'Eleanor Rigby' was McCartney's, but Lennon was also involved in the eventual recorded version.

McCartney has always maintained that the name of the main character in the song was inspired by the name above a shop, but it has been suggested that there is a gravestone in a Liverpool cemetery belonging to someone called Eleanor Rigby, while there is similar doubt about the Father McKenzie character in the song. This is undoubtedly one of the most mature Beatles songs, with an effective string section of session musicians creating a memorable piece of music, which was covered by both Aretha Franklin and Ray Charles, a considerable accolade.

The flip side of the single, 'Yellow Submarine', was a completely different item, although Lennon and McCartney also wrote it. The idea was to provide Ringo Starr with a song on which he could be lead vocalist, and this children's song with a sing-along chorus has become a great favourite. It later became the title song of a cartoon feature film that is usually regarded as the third of the five Beatles movies.

Released as a double A-sided single in the UK, 'Eleanor Rigby'/'Yellow Submarine' topped the chart for a month, while in the US, 'Yellow Submarine' peaked in the Top 3, and simultaneously 'Eleanor Rigby' just failed to reach the Top 10.

There were other excellent songs on 'Revolver', with which other acts scored hits. 'Here, There And Everywhere' is one of McCartney's most pleasing songs, and ten years later it was a hit on both sides of the Atlantic for the Queen of Country/Rock, Emmylou Harris. McCartney was also largely responsible for 'Good Day Sunshine', which was covered by The Tremeloes, who had just parted company with their previous front man, Brian Poole, although their version was not a hit. Lennon's lively and pointed 'And Your Bird Can Sing' is also excellent, although it seems to have been forgotten amid the embarrassment of riches on 'Revolver'. The same is also true of 'For No-One', a McCartney song that happily lacks much of the sentimentality that typified

many of his compositions. The French horn solo (by session musician Alan Civil) is perfectly in keeping with the track's overall feel. The penultimate track on what is clearly the best Beatles album up to this point (and which many consider is the best Beatles album of all), is 'Got To Get You Into My Life', a McCartney song with Motown-styled horns, which was covered by British beat group Cliff Bennett & The Rebel Rousers, whose version, produced by McCartney, became a UK Top 10 hit. Had The Beatles released this, or 'Good Day Sunshine', or 'Here There And Everywhere' as singles, the acts that benefited from such great songwriting might have considered themselves unfortunate.

The final track on the album, 'Tomorrow Never Knows', was Lennon's most advanced attempt thus far at psychedelia, and the chaotic sounds of Lennon's voice, apparently using excerpts from the Tibetan Book of The Dead (a favourite hippie 'bible') amplified through a Leslie speaker over backward tapes, sitars and tape loops, created something which would probably sound much more appealing to those in an altered state than in a sober one. If it wasn't exactly a wonderful climax to 'Revolver', it was brief enough (under three minutes) for listeners to attribute its eccentricities to John Lennon's apparent need to experiment whenever he could get away with it – and several of his other songs on the album suggested that he was still capable of the occasional classic.

Another far less palatable event took place during what would turn out to be the final US tour by The Beatles. Mothers were bringing their children, many of whom were crippled and/or mentally retarded, to the group's dressing rooms in the belief that The Beatles could restore their offspring to normality. If The Beatles had ever wondered whether their decision to stop touring after their 29th of August gig at Candlestick Park had been correct, the nauseating thought that some believed they could cure sickness and disease was enough to convince them that the madness had gone far enough.

CHAPTER EIGHT

After a year when the realities of their situation had become all too clear, The Beatles spent the final months of 1966 attempting to restore some sort of normality to their lives. John Lennon went to Germany and Spain to take a non-musical role in an anti-war movie ironically titled 'How I Won The War', another film by Richard Lester, who had directed both 'A Hard Day's Night' and 'Help!'. Lennon played the minor part of Private Gripweed. The movie starred Michael Crawford, Lee Montague and Roy Kinnear; some reviews singled out Lennon for praise, especially as he was visually unrecognizable with short hair and National Health wireframe glasses. Lennon had been wearing contact lenses for some time, but after this, he reverted to these very basic spectacles, and they became a feature of his image during the early 1970s, when he was rarely, if ever, photographed without them.

Paul McCartney was also involved with a film in late 1966, but not as an actor. He was hired to write the score for 'The Family Way', which starred Hayley Mills, Hywel Bennett and Hayley's father, the great John Mills. The movie concerned the trials and tribulations of a young married couple with interfering parents. McCartney was feeling quite sorry for himself at the time, as Jane Asher, who, unlike the wives of the other three Beatles had a career of her own, was frequently away from him working as an actress. George Harrison, on the other hand, spent his newfound spare time learning how to play the sitar, and George and his wife Patti spent time in Bombay with Ravi Shankar, one of the world's most respected players of the instrument.

Ringo seemed content to just hang around, waiting for his colleagues to start recording again. The major event of the latter part of 1966 came in November, when John Lennon first met Japanese avant-garde artist Yoko Ono, who would play a significant part in the rest of his life.

With touring a thing of the past for The Beatles, Lennon, as one of London's most prominent movers and shakers, was at somewhat of a loose end. John Dunbar, the co-owner of Indica Gallery, invited him to attend a preview of Yoko's 'Unfinished Paintings And Objects' show, where he met Yoko and was impressed by her unorthodox ideas, which he found refreshing and humorous. He was still married to Cynthia at the time, but the meeting with Yoko gave him a fresh impetus. At this point, EMI Records released a Beatles compilation LP, 'A Collection of Beatles' Oldies (But Goldies)', which included 13 UK Number One hits, plus 'Michelle', 'Yesterday', and one track which had never previously appeared in Britain, a cover version of 'Bad Boy' by Larry Williams with a Lennon lead vocal, which had been recorded in 1964 on the same day as another Larry Williams song, 'Dizzy Miss Lizzy', which had appeared on the 'Help!' LP. The compilation album, released for the Christmas market, failed to top the UK chart, where it remained for less than three months.

Two weeks later, the group started the recording sessions that would lead to the monumental 'Sergeant Pepper's Lonely Hearts Club Band', an album that for many years was regarded as the finest LP of the rock era, although it is fair to say that, nearly 40 years later, many commentators feel that 'Revolver' is at least equally good, and arguably superior.

The first track from the sessions, ironically, did not end up on the album. 'Strawberry Fields Forever' was a John Lennon song titled after an area of Liverpool. It was released as one side of a double A-sided single in February 1967 with McCartney's 'Penny Lane', which is also the name of a place in Liverpool. While 'Penny Lane' was a fairly straightforward song, producer George Martin used a brass section of trumpets, flutes and piccolos, which transformed it from a piece of pop (albeit with some bizarre lyrics, probably courtesy of Lennon) into the more obviously commercial side of what is probably the best ever single by The Beatles.

'Strawberry Fields Forever' is completely different.

George Martin later reflected: "Strawberry Fields' is one of my favourites. It started out with John, as always, playing the song to me sitting on a stool in front of me strumming an acoustic guitar, and it was a very gentle song, a beautiful song full of this wonderful word imagery, and I loved it. When we came to do the actual track, there was Ringo bashing away and John on his electric guitar, and it became very much heavier than I'd thought, but that was the way John wanted it and the way it evolved, so we did the track that way and finished it. John came back to me a couple of days after the session, and said 'Well, it wasn't really quite what I had in mind when I wrote the song, so could we do it again?' and this was the first time any of The Beatles had ever asked me to recut a track, so I said 'OK', and he said he wanted me to do a score for it, and that he wanted to use some cellos and horns. So we worked out a score and did a completely new track, and that was fine too.

But again he came back to me, and this time said he liked the new one, but he liked the first one again, as well, so I said he couldn't have them both. And he said 'Why not? Let's take the beginning of one and the end of the other one'. So I told him there were two things wrong with that, the first being that they were in completely different keys, and the second that they were at completely different tempos, and he said, 'You can fix it. You know what I like'. Fortunately I was able to mix it – God was on my side, because the difference in pitch, which was a semitone, was the right way, so that by slowing one down and speeding up the other they would be brought more or less into line. So the two did go together, and that was the way it was issued – see if you can spot the join!'

Despite the quality of the single, it somehow failed to top the UK chart, being unable to outsell 'Release Me' by Engelbert Humperdinck, although for once, American record buyers demonstrated better taste – advance orders in the US exceeded a million copies. 'Penny Lane' topped the chart, and 'Strawberry Fields Forever' separately made the Top 10.

The 'Sergeant Pepper' album took well over three months to record, starting before Christmas 1966 and finally ending in early April 1967, which was far longer than it had taken to complete any previous Beatles album. Geoff Emerick, the engineer who worked with George Martin, maintained that while the 'Please Please Me' album was completed in 585 minutes (under ten hours) from start to finish, 'Sergeant Pepper' took around 700 hours. George Martin said, 'The Beatles definitely had an eternal curiosity for doing something different'. Perhaps the first innovation was the suggestion by McCartney that they should approach the album not as The Beatles, but as a different group, hence Sergeant Pepper's Lonely Hearts Club Band.

The first two songs on the album, the title track and 'With A Little Help From My Friends', were both written initially by McCartney, who sang lead on the title track, which was reprised on the penultimate track of the album. Ringo Starr (introduced by Paul as 'Billy Shears') sang lead on the second track, which follows the opener without the usual silent gap, and this concept was continued throughout the album.

While Ringo's lead vocals are fine (and this was, after all, the original version), Joe Cocker recorded a brilliant cover version, which topped the UK chart, and it became his theme tune, especially after his fantastic performance of the song at the Woodstock Festival in 1969.

This segued into John Lennon's 'Lucy In The Sky With Diamonds', on which he also sang lead. Lennon always maintained that he got the idea for the song when his son, Julian, brought home a painting he had done at school, and when asked what it was meant to be had replied that it was Lucy in the sky with diamonds. Although this could be true, much doubt was cast on this explanation when it was noticed that the initial letters of the three nouns in the title – LSD – were also the initials of a psychedelic drug which was very popular at the time, and as the song's lyrics included such unlikely items as 'tangerine trees and marmalade skies', 'rocking horse people' eating 'marshmallow pies' and 'plasticine porters with looking glass ties', the LSD theory could be correct. McCartney, who sings lead, mainly wrote the fourth song, 'Getting Better', and while it's not bad, it pales in comparison with its three predecessors. 'Fixing A Hole', also written by Paul, is arguably even worse. 'She's Leaving Home' was a third consecutive McCartney song, and while it possesses some redeeming features, this story of a girl deciding to move away from her parents (apparently suggested to Paul by a story he read in the 'Daily Mirror') was described by George Martin as 'one of the biggest hurts of my life'. Martin was working with Cilla

Black when Paul asked him to write an orchestral score for the song, and the producer asked whether McCartney could wait for one day, but the latter was so impatient that he hired Mike Leander (who later successfully worked with Gary Glitter) to write the score. 'Being For The Benefit Of Mr. Kite' was a John Lennon song on which he also sang lead, and it was suggested by a poster Lennon had bought in an antique shop, and is a typically quirky end to the first side of the album.

Side two starts with 'Within You, Without You', a lengthy George Harrison song he wrote on a harmonium, and on which he sings lead. It was recorded with several Indian instruments and violins and cellos, and none of the other Beatles appear on the track, which ends with a burst of laughter, intended by Harrison to provide some light relief after five minutes of sad Indian music.

The next track, 'When I'm 64', was a McCartney special, about which Lennon commented that he had nothing to do with. 'I would never dream of writing a song like that. There are some areas I never think about, and that's one of them.' Lennon did supply backing vocals and guitar to the recording, which is certainly more interesting than its immediate predecessor. 'Lovely Rita', another McCartney song, was about a parking warden, or as McCartney put it, a 'meter maid', an American expression he had heard from an acquaintance. Parking meters had recently been introduced to London, but the song is hardly a masterpiece.

Next comes 'Good Morning, Good Morning', a Lennon song apparently inspired by a TV advert for corn flakes. Once again, this has not stood the test of time very well, and it is interesting that after 35 years quite a lot of 'Sergeant Pepper' seems somewhat trivial. That word cannot be applied to the rocking reprise of the title track, in which The Beatles show that they have not forgotten their roots, nor to the final 'A Day

STEREO

In The Life', a song which starts and ends with passages written and sung by Lennon, while McCartney contributes the middle. Lennon got the idea for the seemingly obscure lyrics from two stories he read in the 'Daily Mail', one concerning Tara Browne, the heir to the Guinness fortune, who was killed in a car crash (although he didn't 'blow his mind out in a car'), while the other was about the fact that the streets of Blackburn in Lancashire contained 4000 holes. The track ends with what Lennon wanted to sound like the end of the world, and there have been many descriptions of how this explosive sound was created. The other remarkable thing about 'Sergeant Pepper' was the packaging. The group was pictured on the front of the sleeve dressed in satin costumes designed by Bermans, the noted theatrical costumiers, and were pictured surrounded by a picture montage of over 50 people with some other paraphernalia in front of them.

The picture montage was intended to include pictures of people whom the group liked. These included black magician Aleister Crowley, film stars Mae West, W. C. Fields, Tony Curtis and Marilyn Monroe, footballers, novelists, explorers, other music stars like Bob Dylan and Dion DiMucci and several whose identities still seem to remain a mystery. The back of the album sleeve also featured the lyrics to every song on the record, something which had never been done before, while inside the sleeve was a sheet of card with cut-outs of a moustache, a picture of Sergeant Pepper, and two badges.

Nearly everything about this album was original – and the fuss was seen to be justified when it topped the UK chart for 22 weeks, selling half a million copies in a month, which was regarded at the time as incredible, although by today's standards, it is not remarkable. The release of 'Sergeant Pepper's Lonely Hearts Club Band' in June was one of the iconic events of 1967…

CHAPTER NINE

Just a month after the release of 'Sergeant Pepper', The Beatles were involved in a groundbreaking television spectacular. 'Our World' was the first live TV show to be broadcast via satellite over 26 countries in front of an estimated audience of 400 million viewers. The Beatles were the only possible choice to represent the era's popular music, and they certainly rose to the occasion, appropriate for the start of a technological advance we now take for granted.

Lennon & McCartney wrote a special song for this groundbreaking extravaganza, which included contributions from many distant corners of the world. Clearly due to the fact that The Beatles were the most popular pop/rock stars of the time, they had to be chosen as the British representatives, and happily, they took their responsibility seriously, although we should not forget that exposure to 400 million viewers probably entered the equation.

'All You Need Is Love' was, and is, a masterpiece, and the 'Our World' sequence was filmed in Abbey Road Studios. The initial backing track for the song had been completed three weeks before the broadcast, and on the day of the filming, The Beatles, who played and sang live, were joined by pairs of trumpeters, trombone players and saxophonists, a squeeze box, four fiddles and two cellos. Lennon's lead vocal is perfect, and in almost every way, the single was perfect, although perhaps the recording's use of snatches of the French national anthem (the Marseillaise), Glenn Miller's 'In The Mood', 'Greensleeves' and 'She Loves You' was

a mistake. However, the footage of the completion of the song was breathtaking with a who's who of contemporary superstars joining in the chorus: Mick Jagger & Keith Richards, Marianne Faithfull, Jane Asher, Patti Harrison, Keith Moon, Graham Nash, among others. It entered the UK chart at Number One, staying at the top for a month, and sold a million in the USA, where it also topped the chart, while even its B-side, the far inferior 'Baby You're A Rich Man', separately (and briefly) reached the US Top 40. This apparently started life as two songs (one each by John and Paul) and was originally scheduled to be part of the soundtrack for the 'Yellow Submarine' movie cartoon.

Less than two months after their triumph in 'Our World', the bottom fell out of the world of The Beatles when their manager, Brian Epstein, was found dead in his bed, apparently from a drug overdose. It is probably true to say that from this point on, without Epstein's judgement to curb their excesses, The Beatles became inconsistent – they could, and did, veer from inspiration to self-indulgence, a good example being their next project. With spare time on their hands, The Beatles showed an endearing desire to be productive, and announced that they would complete a new concept, the 'Magical Mystery Tour'. They had previously discussed this with Epstein, and it would be filmed during that summer and premiere on BBCTV in Britain at Christmas.

The first aspect of the event came in late November, when a single was released of 'Hello Goodbye', an impressive McCartney song on which he sang lead, with a flip side of 'I Am The Walrus', an extraordinary Lennon song whose lyrics make very little sense but are certainly engaging. 'I Am The Walrus' was the first 'Magical Mystery Tour' song to be released, but everyone became familiar with its bizarre qualities prior to the release of the other 'Magical Mystery Tour' songs, because the 'Hello Goodbye' single topped the UK chart for six weeks.

For some reason, the decision was made to release the six songs from 'Magical Mystery Tour' as a double EP in the UK, with a 24-page booklet as part of the package. One of the major problems relating to the 'Magical Mystery Tour' visual experience was that it was filmed in colour, at a time when only a very small percentage of the British populace had access to a colour television.

In colour (which many more people saw in the succeeding decade), 'Magical Mystery Tour' was much more interesting than when it was first screened to universal criticism (and not just by critics, but by almost everyone) on Boxing Day 1967. The insubstantial plot followed The Beatles and a coachload of other people being driven around Cornwall and an airfield at West Malling in Kent. Aboard the coach were the celebrated Scottish eccentric Ivor Cutler, an elderly music hall star named Nat Jackley, and several dwarves. Also Paul McCartney's brother, Mike McGear, and Alexis Mardas, an inventor who would become involved with The Beatles when they launched their own business, Apple Corps. The coach also picked up Spencer Davis in Cornwall, where he was on holiday with his family. Much of the film was surreal, such as a passage in which actress Jessie Robins (who plays the part of Ringo's corpulent Aunt Jessie) sits at a table while John Lennon (playing the part of a waiter) shovels spaghetti on it. Victor Spinetti, who had appeared in both 'A Hard Day's Night' and 'Help!' was also in 'Magical Mystery Tour', but the entire event was alarmingly self-indulgent. One cannot be sure whether it might have been improved if Brian Epstein had been alive to curb the glaring excesses of an idea that clearly lacked direction.

The six musical tracks had been recorded in advance, including the title song, an inspired McCartney composition. In fact, McCartney was responsible for three of the six tracks on the double EP. 'Your Mother Should Know' was very much in the vein of 'When I'm 64', and the gentle 'The Fool On The Hill' has been cited by knowledgeable music commentators as the opposite of Lennon's maniacal 'I Am The Walrus'. There's a rather morose George Harrison song, 'Blue Jay Way', titled after a street in Hollywood where he and Patti had stayed. Finally, there's an instrumental. 'Flying' was the first song credited to all four Beatles.

Overall, 'Magical Mystery Tour' could be termed an over-ambitious failure with a couple of redeeming features in the title track and 'I Am The Walrus'. Apart from music by The Beatles, many felt that one of the more interesting sequences of the entire project was filmed in London's Raymond Revue Bar (a famous night club) in which The Bonzo Dog Doo Dah Band (fronted by Vivian Stanshall and including Neil Innes) played a curious song titled 'Death Cab For Cutie', as a stripper performed.

In the US, Beatle fans were more fortunate than their British counterparts. The Americans weren't at all interested in a double EP, so they added five extra tracks to the six from the film and made it a proper LP. To appreciate just how much luckier they were, it is worth noting that the five extra tracks were 'Penny Lane', 'Strawberry Fields Forever', 'Hello Goodbye', 'All You Need Is Love' and 'Baby You're A Rich Man', the last of which was the only track of the five which was perhaps a little below par.

The additional tracks made the 'Magical Mystery Tour' a highly desirable album that topped the US chart for two months. Of course, the double EP was also a Number One item, but as there were no other double EPs in competition with it, this was a somewhat hollow success.

CHAPTER TEN

Following the death of Brian Epstein, The Beatles decided to form a company to oversee all their various endeavours. The plan was that it wasn't merely music, although they had already launched their own label, Apple Records. An Apple logo had appeared on the 'Magical Mystery Tour double EP, although The Beatles themselves could not be signed to Apple, as they were contracted to EMI/Parlophone – but, among other things, there was an electronics division, a recording studio and a boutique in London's Baker Street, which opened in early December 1967.

In February 1968, all four group members and their wives/girl friends travelled to Rishikesh in India to study transcendental meditation with Maharishi Mahesh Yogi, along with other celebrities, including Mike Love of The Beach Boys, Donovan and film star Mia Farrow, who was there with her sister, Prudence. Ringo was not impressed by the somewhat Spartan conditions at the Maharishi's academy, describing it as 'just like Butlins' and complaining that the food was too spicy, before leaving after only two weeks, while the others remained.

The trip was eventually overshadowed when it became clear that the supposedly holy Maharishi was suspected of using his personal celebrity to extract sexual favours from the young attractive female members of his classes, and the Lennons and Harrisons hurried back to Britain. It should be noted that the Maharishi had never claimed to

be celibate, but Lennon in particular was unhappy with the guru's behaviour. When Lennon told the Maharishi that he and Cynthia and George and Patti were leaving, and was asked why, he said that if the Maharishi was so cosmic and omniscient, he would already know, to which there was no answer.

Back in the UK, the supermodel Twiggy had seen a young Welsh vocalist named Mary Hopkin on a TV talent show, and recommended that Paul McCartney consider signing her to Apple Records. McCartney investigated and agreed that Ms. Hopkin was a potential star, the end result being that her debut single, 'Those Were The Days', the first Apple Records single release, topped the UK chart and reached the US Top 3. It wasn't the only hit single released by Apple, but after such a successful start, the only way to go was downwards.

Meanwhile, The Beatles released a new single in March 1968, 'Lady Madonna'/'The Inner Light'. The A-side, written by McCartney, featured a honky-tonk piano introduction, which many journalists likened to the similar intro to 'Bad Penny Blues', a 1956 single by jazz trumpeter Humphrey Lyttleton. When the great Fats Domino recorded a cover version of 'Lady Madonna' produced by Richard Perry, Perry reported that Domino didn't understand the song's lyrics until he was rehearsing the song and suddenly exclaimed that he loved the song – because he had a daughter named Donna!

On the recording of the song by The Beatles, four jazz saxophonists play, one of whom was Ronnie Scott, founder of the famous jazz club in London's Soho, with McCartney playing bass as well as piano and taking lead vocals. The single deservedly topped the charts on both sides of the Atlantic, although few probably rated the flipside. 'The Inner Light' was the first George Harrison composition released in single form, as this was an extremely Indian-oriented track recorded at EMI Studios in Bombay by Harrison, with his lead vocal, as well as harmony vocals by Lennon & McCartney, added in England.

Strangely, the next project involving The Beatles eventually resulted in a new album, although it was not the next Beatles album released. Even more strangely, following this occurrence, the group made another new album, but history repeated itself, and before that album was released, another one was recorded and released.

The first of these albums to be recorded was a soundtrack album to an animated cartoon feature film based on 'Yellow Submarine', the song that had appeared on the 'Revolver' album. The Beatles make a brief appearance at the end of the film, but otherwise they are portrayed as cartoon characters. Four new songs were recorded by the group for the film, which also used several existing tracks. Apart from 'Yellow Submarine' itself, 'Eleanor Rigby', 'When I'm 64', 'Lucy In The Sky With Diamonds', 'All You Need Is Love', 'Sergeant Pepper's Lonely Hearts Club Band' and an edited version of 'A Day In The Life' were heard on the film soundtrack, although only 'Yellow Submarine' and 'All You Need Is Love' appeared on the soundtrack album, which was not released until six months after the premiere of the movie, perhaps so as not to divert attention from the genuinely new Beatles album which was being recorded around this time.

The four new songs written for the film were 'It's All Too Much', 'Only A Northern Song' (both by George Harrison), McCartney's 'All Together Now' and Lennon's 'Hey Bulldog', while an additional seven tracks on the album were instrumentals composed by George Martin. It probably goes without saying that this is the least essential, original Beatle album. Of the four new songs on

the soundtrack album, 'Hey Bulldog' bizarrely does not appear in the film. The song was apparently completed from start to finish in one day in February 1968, and included the words 'Hey Bullfrog'. McCartney decided to make Lennon laugh by barking, and the sound was captured on tape and retained in the recording, at which point, the song was retitled 'Hey Bulldog'.

'Only A Northern Song' got its title when Harrison was asked to write another song, as the producer, Al Brodax, felt that film was a song short. Harrison apparently gave the swiftly completed song to Brodax with the words 'Here, Al. It's only a northern song'. For once, McCartney's contribution is the best of the bunch, although 'All Together Now' is hardly a masterpiece.

'It's All Too Much', which lasts over six minutes, starts with feeding back guitar and includes a quote from 'Sorrow', a 1966 UK Top 5 hit for The Merseys, another contemporary Liverpool group. It also features a ridiculously long and irrelevant fade.

The plot of the film concerns The Beatles fighting to defend their home, Pepperland, against The Blue Meanies, monsters dedicated to destroying music. From a cinematic point of view, 'Yellow Submarine' probably worked well, but perhaps it was a disappointment musically, especially considering it involved The Beatles.

Of course, the album wasn't released until six months after the movie appeared, and in the meantime, The Beatles released one of their greatest singles, 'Hey Jude'/'Revolution', which was the group's first single to be released with an Apple Records label, although it still bore a Parlophone catalogue number, as The Beatles were contracted to EMI's Parlophone label. 'Hey Jude', which lasts over seven minutes, was previewed on David Frost's

'Frost On Sunday' American TV show, and like 'Our World' was broadcast in Britain via satellite. It was filmed in EMI and Trident Studios with a 40-piece orchestra. Once again, this was basically a McCartney composition, which John Lennon later said he felt was the best song McCartney ever wrote.

'Hey Jude' remained at Number One in Britain for three weeks, after which it was overtaken by a genuine Apple Record, Mary Hopkin's 'Those Were The Days', which had been produced by McCartney. In the USA, 'Hey Jude' remained at Number One for nine weeks, and it also topped the charts in much of mainland Europe, Scandinavia, Malaysia and the Far East. It is said to have included one of the longest fades-out in recorded history – four minutes. Nevertheless, this is one of the greatest Beatle songs ever, with a massively contagious, repetitive chorus.

The story goes that the song was written by McCartney to cheer up Julian Lennon, who was understandably feeling unhappy due to the fact that the marriage of his parents was breaking up in favour of Yoko Ono. Originally 'Hey Jules', it was changed to 'Hey Jude'. The flip side of the single, 'Revolution', was a John Lennon composition, which he had written in India. Several versions of the song were recorded, some lasting as long as ten minutes, but this was the first version released in Britain, although two more versions would appear two months afterwards. The lyrics are interesting: 'We don't want to change the world', sings Lennon, who wants to be 'counted out of destruction' and in terms of contributions to change, 'we are doing what we can'. Within a matter of weeks, Lennon's public image would seem to have changed markedly, as he and Yoko did seem to want to change the world.

Early August 1968 saw sessions commence for the genuine follow-up album to 'Sergeant Pepper'.

"None of us wanted to be the bass player. In our minds he was the fat guy who always played at the back."

Paul McCartney

CHAPTER ELEVEN

November 1968 saw the first solo album by any of The Beatles, a somewhat tedious and uninspired George Harrison project titled 'Wonderwall Music'. It was the soundtrack to an equally tedious and uninspired movie, albeit with a cast which included Jane Birkin, Irene Handl and Richard Wattis. Later in the same month, 'Wonderwall' was virtually forgotten, because the new Beatles album appeared, simply titled 'The Beatles'. Not just an album, but a double album including 30 tracks and lasting over 93 minutes.

The opener, 'Back In The USSR', written and sung by McCartney and clearly with some kind of inspiration from The Beach Boys (remember Mike Love had also been in India with the Maharishi?), was an excellent start, with a nod to Chuck Berry.

'Dear Prudence' was also written in India, but this time by John Lennon, and concerns Mia Farrow's sister, Prudence. Apart from perhaps being a target for the holy man's lust, Prudence apparently spent longer meditating than anyone else. Not a bad track, but not outstanding. Lennon's 'Glass Onion' was more interesting in that its lyrics referred to a number of other recent Beatle songs, including 'Strawberry Fields Forever', 'I Am The Walrus' (he sings that 'The walrus was Paul', although he later claimed that he himself was the walrus, suggesting that he used the word Paul to complete a rhyming couplet), 'Lady Madonna', 'Fool On The Hill' and 'Fixing A Hole'. The song is hardly tuneful, but due to its apparent lyrical Beatle mythology, it is engaging.

Next comes McCartney's slice of Liverpudlian ska 'Ob-La-Di, Ob-La-Da', which made up in contagion for what it lacked in subtlety. The song provided Scottish group Marmalade with their first million-seller and their only UK Number One and was also a UK Top 20 success for one-hit wonders The Bedrocks. Probably the most obviously commercial track on the double album, neither this nor any other track was released as a single on either side of the Atlantic.

By this time, Lennon and McCartney were not writing together as they had before, as evidenced, perhaps, by McCartney's extremely trivial and brief throwaway 'Wild Honey Pie', which surely had nothing at all to do with Lennon, and is of little significance. Lennon's repetitive 'The Continuing Story Of Bungalow Bill' was supposedly inspired (if that's the right word) by a white big game hunter he met in Africa, and it includes a line in the last verse that is supposedly sung by Yoko Ono. Its anti-violence stance cannot be faulted, and its jaunty end includes whistling and applause, but once again, this is hardly a masterpiece.

Fortunately, things improve with the first George Harrison song on the album, 'While My Guitar Gently Weeps', on which Harrison invited his friend Eric Clapton to play the guitar solo. A few years later, Clapton fell in love with George's wife, Patti, and she left Harrison and married Clapton after he was inspired to write 'Layla' about their relationship.

The final track on the first side of the double LP was another Lennon. 'Happiness Is A Warm Gun' was apparently inspired by a phrase in a gun magazine. Its opening passage seems to have little to do with the impressive chorus, and it is hard to understand the line 'Mother Superior jumped the gun', but McCartney later said that this was his favourite Lennon track on the album, while Lennon

considered it a good piece of work. So seven of the first eight tracks on the album were worthwhile.

Unfortunately, this standard was not maintained. Side two starts with 'Martha My Dear', a McCartney song, written about his Old English sheepdog. According to one visitor to McCartney's house, the dog was either not house-trained or was allowed to answer the call of nature inside the house, with predictably unpleasant results. The garden was similarly full of piles of waste products. This has nothing to do with the song, which is a pleasant ballad with McCartney on piano.

It has been said that Lennon's 'I'm So Tired' was along similar lines to his 'I'm Only Sleeping' from 'Revolver', with its memorable chorus about wanting 'a little peace of mind', and the even more memorable lines 'Curse Sir Walter Raleigh, He was such a stupid git', as Lennon smoked yet another cigarette.

From there to another McCartney classic 'Blackbird'. Whether this was some sort of gesture of support for black power activism as has been suggested, is uncertain, but this is very well done and even has sound effects of a bird – presumably a blackbird – singing.

Next comes another George Harrison song 'Piggies', which seems to be about his distaste for the upper classes and the way they behave. Engineer Chris Thomas, later a notable record producer of The Pretenders, Procol Harum and The Sex Pistols, among many others, but then working as George Martin's assistant, plays harpsichord, while once again, sound effects are used, this time of pigs snorting. McCartney's 'Rocky Raccoon' was apparently written in India with the help of Donovan, and McCartney sings in a cod American accent, with George Martin playing honky-tonk piano on what has been described as 'a Mack Sennett

movie set to music'. Sennett was the man behind the wacky Keystone cops film comedies, although it is fair to say that 'Rocky Raccoon' isn't anything like as amusing as the Keystone cops.

'Don't Pass Me By' is Ringo's first solo songwriting success, and it's a country-ish sounding tune which he also sings, with a session fiddle player prominent. Not at all bad for a first try. 'Why Don't We Do It In The Road' sounds like the title of a Lennon song, but it is actually McCartney, who wrote it, played all the instruments and sings. Lennon later called it 'one of Paul's best', although he may have been speaking ironically.

Much better is another McCartney song, 'I Will', which is extremely well done and hard to criticise. If 'Why Don't We Do It In The Road' was untypical of McCartney, then certainly the final track on side two of the double LP 'Julia' is most unlike the majority of Lennon songs of this period. Written about his late mother, this is an emotional song that Yoko Ono helped him to write, and apparently contains lyrics inspired by the Persian poet, Khalil Gibran. Of the nine tracks on the second side of the album, only four or five are better than average.

Side three is a slight improvement. 'Birthday', a rare Lennon & McCartney collaboration at this stage, is a noisy rave up, with both songwriters sharing lead vocal, and Yoko Ono and Patti Harrison among the backing vocalists. 'Yer Blues' is Lennon in blues format, although the lyrics are not really as authentic-sounding as the music. It has been said that he was attacking the somewhat ersatz British blues boom of the late 1960s, but he invited one of the leaders of that movement, Eric Clapton, to perform a live version of the song with him. It was recorded in Toronto, Canada, in September 1969, and included on The Plastic Ono Band's album 'Live Peace In Toronto 1969'. The Plastic Ono Band comprised Lennon, Yoko Ono, and other musicians they invited to participate at various gigs.

Next comes a typically gentle and typically pleasant McCartney song, 'Mother Nature's Son', but the impression is growing that in these latter Beatles days, McCartney's relevance to raucous rock'n'roll was declining, as maturity replaced rebellion. Unfortunately, this led to his influence with the group's original audience becoming less and less – it was difficult to choose between Lennon's apparently increasing eccentricity and McCartney's equally increasing lack of adventure. From this point onwards, with occasional exceptions like Lennon's 'Imagine' and McCartney's 'Band On The Run', these directions were continued.

The sleeve of the double album was completely blank on laminated white card, with the group's name, also in white, embossed (hence the nickname 'the White Album'), and the only print on the sleeve a unique number, as if the album was a limited edition. Of course, the idea of a Beatles product being a limited edition was quite ludicrous.

Lennon's 'Everybody's Got Something To Hide Except Me And My Monkey' is fairly pointless and seems throwaway (although curiously, it was covered by The Ramsey Lewis Trio on a 1969 instrumental LP totally made up of Beatle tunes). 'Sexy Sadie' is another Lennon song and is said to be about the Maharishi, although Lennon was concerned about the possible repercussions of mentioning him by name. The track is interesting both from that point of view and to some extent, musically. 'Helter Skelter' has McCartney sounding like hard rockers such as Robert Plant or Ian Gillan, and this is an excellent, if somewhat chaotic track. Apparently, McCartney had read a review of a record by The Who that was said to be the loudest and most raucous track they had ever recorded, and for some reason, McCartney decided that The Beatles should do something that provoked a similar review. The original recording lasted

24 minutes but was happily edited down to less than five. At the end, Ringo can be heard shouting 'I've got blisters on my fingers!'

This track later became notorious when mass murderer Charles Manson claimed that the lyrics of this song contained instructions from The Beatles for him to kill movie star Sharon Tate and several others. Supposedly, 'Rocky Raccoon' would lead The Black Panthers (a political group) to wipe out the 'Piggies', but this was, of course, total fantasy. Manson remains in prison 43 years later.

The final track on side three of the double album, 'Long, Long, Long' is a George Harrison song that fortunately (and curiously) does not appear to be at all Indian, although the track starts better than its over-ethereal end. Of the seven tracks on side three, three are definitely worthwhile and several of the remaining four are OK, if not outstanding.

The length of time taken to record the 30 tracks on 'The Beatles' was well over four months (30th May to 17th October), although during this period, the group also recorded the 'Hey Jude'/'Revolution' single, and worked on other projects. If the first three sides of the double album were patchy, the fourth side gave rise to the often-expressed opinion about many subsequent double albums – that there were enough good tracks for a single LP, and that the rest should have been rejected as below standard.

Side four starts off well enough with 'Revolution 1', another version of the song already released as the flip side of the 'Hey Jude' single, but this time played more slowly, with backing vocals by Lennon, McCartney and Harrison in the style of 1950s doo-wop music. 'Honey Pie' is a McCartney song ostensibly about a 'Northern working girl' who 'makes it big' in America. This is arranged in the style of a dance band of the 1930s with a saxophone section, and is well done. 'Savoy Truffle' is a most curious George Harrison song that mentions the names of many of the chocolates found in a popular brand of the time, known as 'Week End'.

He was apparently inspired to write the song as a cautionary tale for Eric Clapton, who was unable to resist treating himself to frequent boxes of 'Week End', which George felt would be rotting his friend's teeth.

The nursery-rhyme-like 'Cry Baby Cry' is one of John Lennon's least substantial songs, although it sounds almost significant when compared with Lennon's 'Revolution 9', a sound collage lasting an interminable eight minutes and fifteen seconds, which has little if anything to do with the other two 'Revolution' recordings. The only aspect of it that is memorable is a voice which says 'Number nine' several times at the start.

Finally, 'The Beatles' ends with another Lennon song, 'Goodnight', which he wrote for Ringo to sing. Unexpectedly gentle, it becomes soporific, so perhaps achieves its desired effect of a lullaby.

" Time you enjoy wasting, was not wasted. "

John Lennon

CHAPTER TWELVE

The next Beatle record to be released was the 'Yellow Submarine' LP, although why it was delayed for so long after the film is not clear. It would perhaps never have been as successful in chart terms as a 'proper' Beatles album, and when it did surface in January 1969, the double White Album was still at Number One. 'Yellow Submarine' became the second Beatles album to fail to reach Number One. The only previous 'failure' had been the 'Oldies But Goldies' collection.

On the 5th of December 1967, the Apple Boutique, a clothes shop that had apparently been established as a means of spending some of the company's money on an enterprise in keeping with the group's position as leaders in the 'Swinging London' movement, was opened at 94, Baker Street. On the 31st of July 1968, it closed and all remaining stock was given away.

Ringo had appeared as a gardener in 'Candy', a very strange movie whose cast also included James Coburn. On Christmas day 1967, Paul McCartney and Jane Asher announced their engagement. In June 1968, Paul met his future wife, Linda Eastman, for the first time, and on the 20th of July 1968, Jane Asher announced that her relationship with McCartney was finished.

On the 22nd of August 1968, Ringo left the group, apparently due to the generally bad atmosphere, but rejoined a few days later after he had calmed down, while on the same day, Cynthia Lennon sued John for divorce on the grounds of his adultery with Yoko. He did not contest the lawsuit, and the divorce was granted on the 8th of November, three weeks after Lennon and Ono were arrested for use of cannabis. At the end of that month, Lennon and Yoko Ono released an album titled 'Unfinished Music No.1 – Two Virgins', which was completely unlistenable but caused immense controversy because the album sleeve bore a full frontal photograph of the two totally naked. In Britain, EMI Records refused to distribute the album on the grounds of good taste, while in the USA the album was sold in a brown paper bag with just the two heads visible. After the first two solo albums by individual Beatles, the record-buying public must have been praying for the group to get back to what they had done so well. So that was what they tried to do.

In early January 1969 the group assembled at Twickenham Film Studios theoretically to rehearse for a return to live performance, Paul McCartney's idea. The others were not enthusiastic but eventually agreed to play a live concert that would be filmed and made into a TV special. However, they were unable to book their chosen venue, The Roundhouse in North West London's Chalk Farm, at short notice, and agreed to work at Twickenham. The project was called 'Get Back', and the idea was for the group to return to the way they had been before the immense success they had experienced since early 1963.

By all accounts, the sessions were hard work – George and Paul were constantly bickering, John went everywhere (even to the bathroom!) with Yoko, while Ringo surely must have wondered whether things could ever return to normality. After Ringo's brief departure in August 1968, it was George's turn to leave on the 10th of January 1969, but he returned after five days, after the others promised that the live performance idea would be dropped, but agreeing that a film should be made of the group recording their new album.

During these sessions, tracks were started that would appear on both the last two Beatles studio albums, 'Let It Be' and 'Abbey Road'. On the 20th of January, the decision was made to leave Twickenham studios and to relocate the recordings to the newly installed 72-track recording studio within the Apple building at 3 Savile Row, near Piccadilly Circus in London's West End. This had been designed by 'Magic' Alex Mardas, a Greek inventor, who was well-meaning but whose lack of experience resulted in certain aspects of the studio, such as contact between the control room and the performing space, being unusable. George Martin and the highly renowned studio engineer Glyn Johns had to set up a makeshift facility, which fortunately saved the day.

On the 30th of January, The Beatles played their final live concert on the roof of the Apple building, where they recorded and filmed two new songs. Paul McCartney's 'Get Back' and John Lennon's 'Don't Let Me Down' were performed with black American keyboard player Billy Preston. When the single was released in April, the record label credited 'The Beatles with Billy Preston', the first time a guest artist had been credited on a Beatles single.

This is one of the best singles by The Beatles, and the rooftop concert, which was shown on television, made it certain that it would top the UK chart. It stayed there for five weeks. It also topped the chart for five weeks in the US, where 'Don't Let Me Down' separately reached the Top 40. The end of the month (the next day) brought the end of the 'Get Back' sessions, during which component tracks of two albums were recorded.

George Martin recalled the events: "Let It Be' was a very unhappy album, and when we were recording that, I thought it was the end of everything, because everybody was at each other's throats, the boys were all warring amongst each other, nobody would make any decisions, and for the first time, the engineer wasn't my engineer. For 'Let It Be', they brought in Glyn Johns, who was kind of a producer/engineer, and although we got on fine, there was a certain conflict of interests there, so that I don't think anyone was particularly happy during those recordings. It ended up being a very unsatisfactory record because John Lennon, of all people, had said, 'I don't want this album to have any production gimmicks on it at all, I want it to be an honest album'. I asked him what he meant, because I thought our recordings had been honest, and he said, 'I don't want any overdubbing of voices, or any editing. It's got to be like it is, man, a real honest live recording, so let's do it that way'. Now, the original idea for this was a good one, because we were talking about making a live recording of a new album, and the idea was that we would have a lot of songs written by the boys and rehearsed ad nauseam, and then they would have a marvellous performance in front of a live audience, which would be recorded like a live album, which would also be their new album. Then they decided to film it all. So we had camera teams looking over our shoulders all the time – it was an awful mess. And so the only way I could make the album in the end was to make it an honest record and have all the burps and false takes, almost like a documentary, and that was the way I finished it up with Glyn.'

Johns, who was employed on the project more as an engineer than as a producer, and had previously worked with The Beatles on a 1964 TV show, 'Around The Beatles', was approached by Paul McCartney in December 1968: 'He rang me up and said they were going to do a television show that they were going to produce themselves, and they were going to make a documentary film of them making the show; from that, an album would be released of all new material which they were writing for the show which would be recorded live. He wanted me to go along for the rehearsals, and pretty much become involved from Day One, which I did. It was obviously a fascinating experience. I was extremely flattered that they should ask me to work with them. By the time I actually got into a room with them, although I was quite used to working with famous people and was very rarely phased by anyone I met no matter how much I admired them, actually being in a room with The Beatles for the first time – all four of them with nobody else there – was pretty weird. The time I worked with them was at the end of their career, obviously, and the 'Let It Be' thing was something of a fiasco. The extraordinary thing is that they had proved up to that point that they were the masters of the 'produced record', yet the stuff I did with them wasn't 'produced' in that way at all, it was all recorded live in a rehearsal situation.'

As already mentioned, the 'Let It Be' album was not released until May 1970, although virtually all the recording of the tracks had been completed a year earlier.

However, none of The Beatles were especially happy with the album, which was why John Lennon had invited noted American record producer Phil Spector to work on the tapes to produce a finished album. Spector, who had enjoyed many memorable hits during the 1960s with artists like The Ronettes, The Crystals, The Righteous Brothers and Ike & Tina Turner, had made it known that he was anxious to work with The Beatles, and he had been given 'an audition' in late January, 1970. That audition produced 'Instant Karma', a single by The Plastic Ono Band. John Lennon was happy enough with Spector's work, but it took two more months before the other Beatles agreed to let him loose on the 'Let It Be' recordings. The results were generally agreed to be patchy at best. The opening 'Two Of Us', a McCartney ballad, is pleasant and was, by all accounts, written for Mortimer, a teenage group from New York who were signed to Apple, although if they recorded the song, the results have never seen the light of day. Lennon can be heard at the start of the track saying: 'I dig a pigmy by Charles Hawtrey on the deaf aids'. Hawtrey was a well-known British comedy actor, who was in many of the 'Carry On' movies.

Lennon's 'Dig A Pony' has one of the false starts referred to above, and has Billy Preston on electric piano. The song is not outstanding, which was true of many of the songs on this album. One exception may be John Lennon's 'Across The Universe'. The version on the 'Let It Be' album was, in fact, a second version; the original had been recorded in February 1968, one day after 'Lady Madonna', with George playing sitar, with Ringo on drums and coke tin behind Lennon's lead vocal. He and Paul decided that they needed female backing vocalists, and invited two of the girls who were always hanging about outside the recording studio to become famous for fifteen minutes. The track was to be

included on a charity album titled 'No One's Gonna Change Our World', proceeds of which benefited the World Wildlife Fund, dedicated to raising money to prevent species of animals becoming extinct.

The album had been the idea of comedian Spike Milligan, who wrote a sleeve note, as did HRH Prince Philip, and was co-ordinated by George Martin. Other artists who contributed tracks included Cilla Black, Cliff Richard, The Bee Gees, The Hollies and Lulu, and the album was only available for two years. Lennon was apparently not satisfied either with the original recording or the 'Let It Be' version of 'Across The Universe', saying: 'That song was never recorded properly', but claiming it as one of the best songs he had written. Phil Spector had removed the drums, but added a choir and an orchestra, and this was a worthwhile track, despite Lennon's reservations.

'I Me Mine' is a George Harrison song. The lyrics reflect the conflicts that were afflicting both the group and Apple's business in general. 'Dig It', which lasts just 48 seconds, is an example of the documentary approach referred to by George Martin and Glyn Johns. Originally five minutes long, 'Dig it' was composed by all four Beatles, and is at best disposable. A version of the title track follows, but different to the single. McCartney sings lead on one of his best ever compositions – the lyrical reference to 'Mother Mary' has always been presumed to refer to his late mother. Harrison's guitar is played through a Leslie speaker, which makes the sound resemble that of an organ. The main difference between this version and the one released as a single is his excellent guitar solo. 'Maggie Mae' is another fragment, lasting 39 seconds, and is credited as traditional, arranged by the four Beatles. It is an old Liverpudlian song that mentions a famous local thoroughfare, Lime Street, apparently well known for both its station and its ladies of the night. While this isn't exactly the same song as the

'Maggie Mae' with which Rod Stewart topped the charts in 1972, there are similarities.

McCartney wrote the early part of 'I've Got A Feeling', and Lennon the latter. Despite the fact that both were involved, this is hardly a masterpiece.

'One After 909' is an old Lennon song, apparently written in 1959, and he ends it by singing a line from the Irish chestnut, 'Danny Boy'.

Following this is one of the best moments of the whole album, McCartney's 'The Long And Winding Road', to which Phil Spector added a full orchestra and choir. By the way, the 'long and winding road' alluded to in the song is sometimes claimed to have been inspired by the B842, a thirty-one mile (50 km) winding road in Scotland.

Although McCartney made it clear that he was not impressed by Spector's work, he was not heard protesting when it was released as a single in the US where it topped the chart.

The penultimate track on the 'Let It Be' album was George Harrison's 'For You Blue', on which John Lennon plays slide guitar, provoking lead vocalist George to ironically remark, 'Elmore James got nothing on this'. For the uninitiated, James was a noted blues guitarist who was an influence on many groups, including Fleetwood Mac, during the blues boom of the mid-1960s. Again with no discernible Indian leanings, this track is OK.

Finally, 'Get Back' (like 'Let It Be', a slightly different version from the chart-topping single release), which includes Lennon's jocular remark 'Sweet Loretta fart, thought she was a cleaner, but she was a frying pan'. Not as good as the single version, but this is one of Paul McCartney's best compositions, and his lead vocal also cannot be faulted. The 'Let It Be' film, which was supposed to document the making of the album, was tedious to the point of being virtually unwatchable. In 2003, the surviving Beatles and Yoko Ono released 'Let It Be… Naked', which was claimed to be the way they wanted the album to sound. McCartney said that the reason for this was that he had been unhappy with the original album for over 30 years, and in particular with the released version of 'The Long and Winding Road'.

The new version included no other instruments than those used in the studio when the track was originally recorded.

As it turned out, the release of the 'Let It Be' album, which was packaged in a slipcase that also contained a book of photographs taken during the record sessions, was the last Beatles release while the group was still working together as a quartet, although it was not the last original album they recorded.

CHAPTER THIRTEEN

During March 1969 both John Lennon and Paul McCartney got married, McCartney to Linda Eastman in London on the 12th, and Lennon to Yoko Ono at the British Consulate in Gibraltar on the 20th. On the 25th of March, Lennon and his new wife flew to Amsterdam, where they staged a week long 'Bed in' at the Hilton hotel to promote world peace. On the 22nd of April, he changed his middle name – John Winston Lennon became John Ono Lennon.

On the 26th of April, 'Get Back'/'Don't Let Me Down' entered the UK chart at Number one. In May, John and Yoko staged another 'Bed in', this time in Montreal, Canada, and at the end of that month, The Beatles released yet another new single. 'The Ballad Of John And Yoko' was a song that had been recorded in mid-April by Lennon and McCartney without the other two group members, who were busy elsewhere. The single reached Number One in the UK, although it is most unlike the vast majority of their singles, and seems to be more of a folk-styled song, in which John Lennon talks about his 'Bed in' activities. This one was hardly made for dancing.

The flip side, George Harrison's 'Old Brown Shoe' (again with no Indian input) is OK without being outstanding.

During the summer of 1969, no new Beatles records appeared, although both John Lennon and George Harrison released solo albums, neither of which were, in truth, any improvement on their earlier solo efforts. Both were released on the short-lived Zapple label. Harrison's 'Electronic

Sound' is exactly that, two sides of electronic sound, one titled 'Under The Mersey Wall' and the other 'No Time Or Space'. Any connection this may have had with music is impossible to discern.

Lennon & Yoko's 'Unfinished Music No.2 – Life With The Lions', also contained too little music, although one side of it did include vague musical sounds, as it was a live recording of a concert titled 'Cambridge 1969', which was where and when it happened. Yoko is vocalist (in what has been described as 'free form style', John plays guitar, while saxophonist John Tchicai and percussionist John Stevens join in.

The second side of the LP is made up of recordings made during Yoko's three weeks in Queen Charlotte's hospital West London, during November 1968, which resulted in a miscarriage. Once again, this is hardly essential listening for Beatles' fans.

A new Plastic Ono Band single 'Give Peace A Chance' was released in early July, which had been recorded during their Montreal 'Bed in'. In many ways, this was a chant more than a song, but it was infinitely preferable to the stuff on the 'Unfinished Music' albums. The single made the UK Top 3 and the US Top 20. Even so, it wasn't a Beatles record.

The final original Beatles album, 'Abbey Road', surfaced in late September 1969.

George Martin recalled: 'A few months after the 'Let It Be' sessions, Paul rang me up and said, 'Look, I'm a bit fed up with the way things have been going. Will you come back and produce an album like you used to?'. I said 'Well, Paul, I don't know whether it will work. I'd love to if I'm able to, but in order for me to be able to do that, you've got to want to be produced, and you've got to do what I say'. He said they'd do that, and I said I wanted to do it at Abbey Road, which he also agreed to, and it was a very happy album. We tried to put aside all the differences, and although it wasn't an integrated album, because everybody was writing their own material and tended to be working mainly on their own songs, for which the others would reluctantly come in, it was a much happier album than I really expected. Paul and I worked very solidly on the second side – John didn't want the production things, which he'd never liked, and the concept things bored him to tears because he liked good old rock'n'roll, so we compromised and put his rock'n'roll things on one side, and the long-winded concept on the other, which was the way it worked out. I knew it was the end of the road, but it was a happy end, and I'm glad it worked out like that. I was considerably shaken when 'Let It Be' was issued after that in the format it was, with Phil Spector's work on it'.

Bearing this in mind, 'Abbey Road' is very much a curate's egg of an album, which opens with Lennon's 'Come Together', one of his very best songs from the end of the group's active career. This song must be familiar, not least as it has been a hit single for Ike & Tina Turner, Aerosmith and Michael Jackson as well as The Beatles and has been covered by, among others, Booker T. & The MGs, Elton John and Chairmen Of The Board. A great song, not least because of its appealing double meaning and sexual connotations.

The tour de force was followed by 'Something', undoubtedly one of George Harrison's best songs, which continues the high standard, and was also the subject of many covers, including by such artists as Shirley Bassey, whose version was a UK Top 5 hit, Frank Sinatra (it was apparently the only Beatles song he ever recorded), Elvis Presley, Joe Cocker, Ray Charles, James Brown and Smokey Robinson and dozens more.

From the sublime to 'Maxwell's Silver Hammer', a somewhat surreal McCartney song that sounds like a cheerful sing-along. The song is actually about a medical student named Maxwell Edison, who commits murders using a silver hammer, his victims being his girlfriend, Joan, his teacher, and the judge during his murder trial.

'Oh Darling' was another McCartney song in which he attempts, with reasonable success, to sound like a soul singer. Apparently, John Lennon resented the fact that his partner did not ask him to sing lead on this song.

The fifth track on the album continued the impressive standard, which some found surprising as it was written and sung by Ringo. While it is hardly a masterpiece, 'Octopus's Garden' is acceptable. The final track on the first side of the LP, 'I Want You (She's So Heavy)', was also the album's longest track at over seven and a half minutes, and Lennon said it was his impassioned love song to Yoko, although, to many ears, it goes on too long, and ends abruptly.

Side two begins with another excellent George Harrison song, 'Here Comes The Sun', on which Harrison uses his recently acquired Moog synthesiser. Steve Harley & Cockney Rebel covered the song in 1976, making it a UK Top 10 hit. The song was written on a sunny day in Eric Clapton's garden, when Harrison was visiting his friend. 'Because' is an unlikely Lennon song he wrote after hearing Yoko Ono play some chords written by Beethoven. Lennon told her to play the chords backwards, and the result became 'Because'.

'You Never Give Me Your Money' was a McCartney song in which he is believed to have been complaining about the parlous state of Apple, and the deteriorating relationships within the group.

The remaining seven listed tracks are virtually a segue lasting over eleven minutes, which suggests that many of these songs were incomplete fragments, like Lennon's

'Sun King', originally titled 'Los Paranoias', which has meaningless lyrics, although it sounds attractive, and his 'Mean Mr. Mustard', written during the time the group spent in India, leading to speculation that the song may be about the Maharishi.

Another Lennon song, 'Polythene Pam', was also written during that Indian visit and is supposedly about (as Lennon put it) 'a mythical Liverpool scrubber dressed up in her jackboots and kilt'.

McCartney's 'She Came In Through The Bathroom Window' tells about how young girl fans used to break into his London home in search of souvenirs. Joe Cocker covered the song in a far superior version.

'Golden Slumbers' is a McCartney ballad that starts with a verse of traditional song he supposedly heard his grandmother sing. This is, once again, an average piece of work. It runs into 'Carry That Weight', another McCartney irrelevance, although he compensates to a certain extent with 'The End', which might be seen as an epitaph, as all four Beatles play solos. The song contains the oft-quoted lyrics 'And in the end, the love you take, is equal to the love you make'.

After a twenty-second gap comes a hidden track, 'Her Majesty', which lasts for just over twenty seconds, and is McCartney's tribute to HRH The Queen, in which calls her 'a pretty nice girl'. A curious end to an album that started with considerable promise but really only contained one classic track on its second side.

Obviously it topped the charts on both sides of the Atlantic and in many other countries, selling several million copies. Apart from the 'Let It Be' LP and single – the latter a great version, superior to the title track of the album – that was the end of The Beatles as an active group. It is unlikely that we will ever see their like in our lifetime.

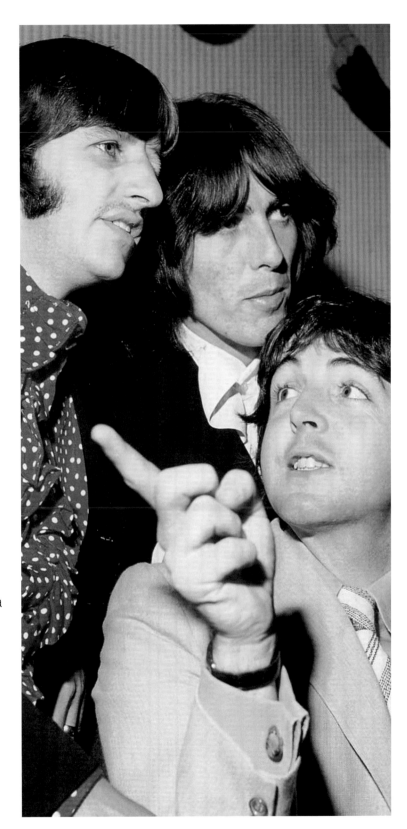

The Beatles In Review:

PLEASE PLEASE ME

With two UK hit singles to their name – 'Love Me Do' having reached Number 17 in late 1962, and 'Please Please Me' on its way to Number 1, in the New Musical Express chart at least – the Beatles faced 1963 in optimistic mood. While record label Parlophone had cautiously sanctioned an album, budget restrictions meant that the bulk of it had to be recorded in a marathon 12-hour session at Abbey Road on the 11th of February 1963 (the two singles and B-sides already in the can). Not even the fact that John Lennon was suffering from a heavy cold was allowed to delay proceedings. The total cost was a miserly £400.

Before 'Please Please Me', which logically took its name from the recent hit, LPs tended to be built around a single or two and padded out with filler. It was without precedent for a group to contribute eight self-written songs, as the Beatles did here (the credits on the label and sleeve are to 'McCartney-Lennon' rather than the more familiar reverse). The hit single that became the album's title track appears not as the opening song but at the end of side one. Even on their first album, the Beatles began to rewrite the rules.

Like many debuts of the era, the album was loosely based around the band's stage act, combining covers and original material. They would dip back into their extensive live repertoire again for future albums. What 'Please Please Me' may lack in polish it makes up for in raw energy and freshness. Not surprisingly, given the tightness of the schedule, no time was allowed for overdubbing.

'Please Please Me' went straight to the top of the album chart and stayed there for 30 weeks, until displaced by its follow-up, 'With The Beatles'. EMI/Parlophone must have been delighted with the return on their investment.

I SAW HER STANDING THERE
(Lennon-McCartney)

Paul's count-in heralds a lively opening track that is, perhaps, the first truly British rock'n'roll song – 'you know what I mean?'

MISERY
(Lennon-McCartney)

'Misery' provides a touch of humour with the band already confident enough to poke fun at themselves. The song was written for touring friend Helen Shapiro, whose producer, Norrie Paramor, turned it down, allowing singer/actor Kenny Lynch to record the first Beatles cover.

ANNA (GO TO HIM)
(Alexander)

This cover version of American R&B artist Arthur Alexander's song is notable for an impassioned vocal from Lennon.

CHAINS
(Goffin-King)

Less successful is this version of a tune originally by Little Eva's backing group, the Cookies. George Harrison's first lead vocal is a little shaky.

BOYS
(Dixon-Farrell)

Inheriting previous drummer Pete Best's solo piece, Ringo dutifully hollers the album's first Shirelles number. Incongruously, the band omitted to change the gender.

ASK ME WHY
(Lennon-McCartney)

The B-side of 'Please Please Me' features a reference back to 'Misery' in a piece mainly written by Lennon in the style of Motown favourites Smokey Robinson and the Miracles.

PLEASE PLEASE ME
(Lennon-McCartney)

Inspired variously by Bing Crosby, Elvis Presley and Roy Orbison, it took the Beatles two attempts to convince producer George Martin of the merits of the song. Speeded up and laden with hooks, the reworked version vindicated Lennon and McCartney as songwriters.

LOVE ME DO
(Lennon-McCartney)

The debut single hints at the greatness to come. Nerves on the occasion of their first studio recording are evident in McCartney's voice.

PS I LOVE YOU
(Lennon-McCartney)

An early example of McCartney's willingness to experiment with structure comes in the form of a letter song, a format inspired by the Shirelles' 'Soldier Boy'.

BABY IT'S YOU
(David-Bacharach-Williams)

The Shirelles connection continues with a version of their Bacharach and David-penned hit. Another convincing Lennon vocal graces the track.

DO YOU WANT TO KNOW A SECRET
(Lennon-McCartney)

Democracy prevails as George sings a Lennon-McCartney original. The song became a UK Number 1 for Billy J. Kramer and the Dakotas, the first of many chart-topping covers of Beatles album tracks.

A TASTE OF HONEY
(Marlow-Scott)

The first recorded example of Paul's predilection for show tunes, this was the title song of the 1961 film version of Shelagh Delaney's play.

THERE'S A PLACE
(Lennon-McCartney)

Written mainly by Lennon but sung largely by McCartney (John's cold is evident on his vocal contributions), 'There's A Place' has one of the album's most interesting and revealing lyrics.

TWIST AND SHOUT
(Russell-Medley)

The allotted 12 hours were up, but George Martin felt they needed another track to close the album with a bang. The stage favourite version of the Isley Brothers' song was recorded in one larynx-shredding take, reaching a level of excitement previously unknown in British rock'n'roll.

WITH THE BEATLES

In the eight months between albums, the Beatles' momentum had become unstoppable. They were now a national phenomenon thanks to constant touring, television and radio appearances, plus two chart-topping singles, 'From Me To You' and the phenomenal 'She Loves You'. 'Beatlemania' had already entered the language following fan hysteria surrounding their appearance on Sunday Night At The London Palladium in October 1963. 'I Want To Hold Your Hand', released a week after 'With The Beatles', would consolidate their status at home and crack the biggest market in the world – America. That the album and single were permitted to stand alone is a testament to the band's phenomenal success in such a short space of time.

The Fab Four continued to innovate. The moody, dramatically half-lit cover photograph was quite different to anything that had come before and would be endlessly imitated and parodied in years to come.

'With The Beatles' repeated the formula of its predecessor, with eight originals and six covers. The sessions were conducted in July, September and October 1963, sandwiched between the group's other commitments.

Some of the rough edges have been rubbed off, and the quartet sound more assured but achieve this without sacrificing any of their vitality. Doubletracking of vocals is used for the first time, an effect that John Lennon was very much taken with.

With advance orders of 270,000, it was inevitable that the album would go straight to Number 1 on its release in November 1963, remaining there for 21 weeks and becoming the first British-recorded LP to sell a million copies in the UK. The vitality and freshness of 'With The Beatles' is undimmed by the passing years, coming closer to capturing the essence of Beatlemania than any other record.

IT WON'T BE LONG

(Lennon-McCartney)

An urgent Lennon opener that features some basic word play ('be long' and 'belong') and a knowing echo of 'She Loves You' in the repeated 'yeah, yeah' refrain.

ALL I'VE GOT TO DO

(Lennon-McCartney)

The tempo slows for this Smokey Robinson-inspired piece, which was written by John in 1961.

ALL MY LOVING

(Lennon-McCartney)

Interviewed shortly before his death, Lennon was generous in his praise of this wonderful McCartney composition and proud of his own contribution, the super-fast guitar triplets that drive it. One of many singles that never were (in Britain at least) 'All My Loving' gained much airplay as the title track of an EP released in February 1964.

DON'T BOTHER ME

(Harrison)

George Harrison makes his songwriting debut on a lightweight effort delivered with customary verve from the band and an improved vocal performance from its composer.

LITTLE CHILD

(Lennon-McCartney)

One minute 45 seconds of vigorous duet between John and Paul.

TILL THERE WAS YOU

(Willson)

The Beatles', and in particular Paul's, range of influences extended beyond rock'n'roll to Broadway musicals such as Meredith Wilson's 1957 play The Music Man from which this song is taken. The version here, replete with George's Spanish guitar solo, is closer to Peggy Lee's reading.

PLEASE MR POSTMAN

(Dobbin-Garrett-Garman-Brianbert)

An urgent reading of the Marvelettes' 1961 American chart-topper.

ROLL OVER BEETHOVEN

(Berry)

Side two of the vinyl LP began with the band celebrating a key influence, Chuck Berry. Sung by Harrison, this version is slightly slower than the original.

HOLD ME TIGHT

(Lennon-McCartney)

The rapidity of early Beatles sessions led to occasional uncorrected errors such as Paul's off-key singing here.

YOU REALLY GOT A HOLD ON ME

(Robinson)

A bravura Lennon vocal distinguishes the Beatles' take on this Smokey Robinson and the Miracles song, which was the first track to be recorded for the album.

I WANNA BE YOUR MAN

(Lennon-McCartney)

The speed at which John and Paul finished this song for them helped inspire Mick Jagger and Keith Richards to write their own material. A simple composition, this gave the Rolling Stones their first Top 20 hit and, reworked for Ringo, provides amiable filler.

DEVIL IN HER HEART

(Drapekin)

The most obscure of the album's covers was originally recorded by the Donays, a US all-girl group. George takes lead vocal with strong backing support from John and Paul.

NOT A SECOND TIME
(Lennon-McCartney)

The extent to which the Beatles had penetrated even the deepest bastions of the British establishment became apparent in the Sunday Times review of 'With The Beatles', in which serious music critic William Mann praised the 'Aeolian cadences' at the end of 'Not A Second Time'. The Beatles found this hilarious, having no idea what they were.

MONEY (THAT'S WHAT I WANT)
(Gordy-Bradford)

The big finish is this time provided by an intense version of the Barrett Strong original and another committed Lennon vocal. The lyrical content is not without irony – the Beatles often made half-joking reference in interviews and press conferences to their monetary ambitions.

A HARD DAY'S NIGHT

Following the established showbiz career trajectory, the next step for the Beatles was to make a film. Neatly side-stepping the pitfalls of the star vehicle, which had damaged Elvis's credibility and done few favours for Cliff Richard, they opted for a semi-realistic approach, centred on the preparations for a live show. In this format, the songs fitted naturally, and the audience was allowed a glimpse into the eye of the storm of Beatlemania, albeit fictionalised.

Directed by Richard Lester (who, like record producer George Martin, had worked with Beatles heroes the Goons) and filmed in grainy black and white, A Hard Day's Night was shot in a frantic seven-week period. It proved to be massively influential – the scene where the Beatles frolic to 'Can't Buy Me Love' virtually invented the Monkees' television show.

The soundtrack is the only Beatles album composed entirely by Lennon and McCartney. Side one features seven songs

from the movie, while the second side contained six more that didn't make the finished cut. American buyers were not so fortunate; the US version contained only eight songs, plus four instrumentals from George Martin's film score.

As a songwriting partnership, Lennon and McCartney's relationship was based as much on competition as collaboration. Many of the early songs had been written, in Lennon's phrase, 'eyeball to eyeball', a practice that all but ceased from now on. With some notable exceptions, the songs display a charmingly naive, romantic allure. Ringo's acting contribution to the movie was justly praised, and while the album lacks his traditional vocal slot, his propulsive drumming is exemplary throughout, never more so than on the title track.

A HARD DAY'S NIGHT

(Lennon-McCartney)

Determined to secure the film's title song, once this Ringo-ism (coincidentally used by Lennon in his book In His Own Write) had been adopted as the name for the project, John wrote the piece overnight, and the band recorded it the very next day. A masterclass of invention from the massive opening chord to the jangling fade.

I SHOULD HAVE KNOWN BETTER

(Lennon-McCartney)

John's writing dominates the LP and his harmonica playing is showcased here. This was the first song to feature in the film, with the band playing it in the guard's van of the train.

IF I FELL

(Lennon-McCartney)

A familiar Lennon theme – fear of betrayal – is central to this affecting composition.

I'M HAPPY JUST TO DANCE WITH YOU

(Lennon-McCartney)

Penned by John in upbeat mode for George to sing.

AND I LOVE HER

(Lennon-McCartney)

A much-covered McCartney acoustic ballad written for actress girlfriend Jane Asher.

TELL ME WHY

(Lennon-McCartney)

Many Beatles songs from this era were written to order and 'Tell Me Why' is one such, created quickly as an uptempo number for the concert sequence of the movie.

CAN'T BUY ME LOVE

(Lennon-McCartney)

Recorded in Paris after taping German-language versions of 'She Loves You' and 'I Wanna Hold Your Hand', 'Can't Buy Me Love' harks back to a previous generation, its jazzy feel cementing the band's all-ages appeal.

ANY TIME AT ALL

(Lennon-McCartney)

Again powered by Ringo's drumming, this vibrant performance hides a standard-issue lyric.

I'LL CRY INSTEAD

(Lennon-McCartney)

The Beatles dip a collective toe into country and western territory for this short but pithy number, which was originally intended for the movie's 'frolicking' scene.

THINGS WE SAID TODAY
(Lennon-McCartney)

Paul's compositions for the project all possessed a distinctive atmosphere, his versatility already evident. This was written while on holiday with Jane Asher, and its reflective feel contrasts nicely with the rest of the album.

WHEN I GET HOME
(Lennon-McCartney)

Another exhilarating rocker, similar in theme to the title track.

YOU CAN'T DO THAT
(Lennon-McCartney)

Influenced, according to John, by American soul singer Wilson Pickett, the lyric reveals the misogynistic side of Lennon's nature for the first time.

I'LL BE BACK
(Lennon-McCartney)

A melancholy but defiant finale, this was one of John's favourites among his early songs.

BEATLES FOR SALE

Two months after completing the previous album, work began on 'Beatles For Sale', which would be completed in the course of three batches of sessions over a four-month period interspersed with foreign tours, including their first full American jaunt. The sessions also produced the single 'I Feel Fine' and its B-side 'She's A Woman', the former being the first riff-driven Beatles single. Both single and LP were aimed squarely at the Christmas market, a fact acknowledged in publicist Derek Taylor's sleeve notes and implicit in the cynical title.

The packaging was unusually lavish for the time, comprising a gatefold sleeve that featured the Fabs against a collage of photographs, which resembled a precursor to 'Sgt. Pepper'. The cover shows the band, hair noticeably longer, unsmiling and tired around the eyes, as if the speed of Beatles life was finally catching up with them.

After the all-original 'A Hard Day's Night', the band were forced to dip back into their reservoir of non-originals to complete the album, reverting to the eight/six ratio of the first two albums. Four of the cover versions were taped, along with other songs, in a lengthy session on the 18th of October 1964.

The infectious joie de vivre of the first three albums is replaced by a more sombre feel, and many of the Lennon-McCartney compositions are

downbeat, suggesting that disillusionment with the treadmill of Beatlemania was seeping into their songwriting. Musically, 'Beatles For Sale' contains no great leaps forward, but the band continue to refine and adapt their sound, remaining, as always, at least two steps ahead of the competition. There were relatively few versions by other artists of the Lennon-McCartney originals from the album, although UK prog-rockers Yes recorded a version of 'Every Little Thing' for their first album in 1969.

Released in December 1964, 'Beatles For Sale' remains an underrated album, perhaps because some of the more perfunctory cover versions appear retrograde steps when compared to some intriguing new material.

NO REPLY
(Lennon-McCartney)
The first of two downcast Lennon scenarios opens the album with a dramatically arranged story of deceit.

I'M A LOSER
(Lennon-McCartney)
Lennon's most significant early lyric features the revealing lines, 'Although I laugh and I act like a clown/beneath this mask I am wearing a frown' and 'I'm not what I appear to be' couched in the familiar territory of a love song.

BABY'S IN BLACK
(Lennon-McCartney)
Venturing further into country music, 'Baby's In Black' lightens the mood with some mordant humour.

ROCK AND ROLL MUSIC
(Berry)
The album's most successful cover breathes new life into the Chuck Berry classic with a powerful Lennon vocal.

I'LL FOLLOW THE SUN
(Lennon-McCartney)
Written by Paul in 1959 and revived in the absence of sufficient new material, this displays typical McCartney optimism, although the callow lyric reveals its age.

MR MOONLIGHT
(Johnson)
An obscure song that was originally the B-side of 'Dr Feelgood' by Dr Feelgood and the Interns (no relation to the later pub-rockers). The Beatles' version is notable for Lennon's committed vocal and McCartney's cheesy Hammond organ solo.

KANSAS CITY/HEY, HEY, HEY, HEY
(Leiber-Stoller) (Penniman)
Paul's definitive Little Richard impression was featured on 'Long Tall Sally', released on EP in June 1964, but this energetic version of a Richard medley isn't far behind. 'Kansas City' was written by Jerry Leiber and Mike Stoller, while the second half of the piece was a Little Richard original.

EIGHT DAYS A WEEK
(Lennon-McCartney)
The most obviously commercial of the material recorded at the session, this was passed over as a single in favour of 'I Feel Fine'. The jangly guitar figure fades the song in and out, while in-between times, John and Paul duet on a near-perfect pop song.

WORDS OF LOVE
(Holly)
Buddy Holly was perhaps the major influence on the Beatles as a performer who wrote his own material and whose backing group helped inspire the band's name. One of his early, less successful singles, 'Words Of Love' was the only Holly song they recorded.

HONEY DON'T

(Perkins)

The first of two Carl Perkins songs tackled by the Beatles for this album, 'Honey Don't' was the B-side of Perkins' original of 'Blue Suede Shoes'. Sung live by John, it provides Ringo's vocal showpiece here as he tries to rally his exhausted colleagues.

EVERY LITTLE THING

(Lennon-McCartney)

Even amid the pressures of their overloaded schedule, the Beatles could still come up with overlooked masterpieces like this, which was probably written by McCartney but sung by Lennon.

I DON'T WANT TO SPOIL THE PARTY

(Lennon-McCartney)

Another mournful country-influenced piece, with the normally defiant John sounding defeated.

WHAT YOU'RE DOING

(Lennon-McCartney)

An early experiment with studio technology, 'What You're Doing' contains an uncorrected vocal mistake at the start but this fails to mar another uncelebrated gem.

EVERYBODY'S TRYING TO BE MY BABY

(Perkins)

Carl Perkins was a major influence on George's guitar playing. Harrison sings this desultory cover of his song, which was recorded in one take.

HELP!

Following 'A Hard Day's Night' was bound to be difficult, and the task was entrusted to the same team behind the earlier film, Dick Lester and producer Walter Shenson. The second of a three-picture deal with United Artists, Help! enjoyed a bigger budget and location filming in the Bahamas and Austria (doubling as a tax dodge), but the final product, shot this time in colour, was an uneasy compromise. The Beatles play themselves in a comedy action romp that is saved from the pitfalls of Elvis movies only by Lester's ahead-of-its-time direction. The Fab Four floated through the shoot in a haze of marijuana smoke, feeling like extras in their own film.

One of the most lasting side effects of the movie was that it sparked George Harrison's enduring interest in all things Indian, which was to exert considerable influence over the music and lives of all the Beatles in the coming years.

Like 'A Hard Day's Night', the album features the movie songs on side one only. Their fifth album in a little over two years, 'Help!' is a schizophrenic exercise. Much of it is perfunctory Beatles-by-numbers, but at its best, the album serves notice that the band were poised to take pop music to new and ever stranger places.

'Help!' effectively marks the end of phase one of the Beatles' career. From now on, the band would start to wrest control of its destiny from EMI, Brian Epstein and 'the men in suits' who had exploited Beatlemania for the previous two years. This process would result in their undoing at the end of the decade, but would coincide with the band's most creative period.

HELP!

(Lennon-McCartney)

Resolved again to claim the title song of the film once the unwieldy working title 'Eight Arms to Hold You' had been discarded, Lennon quickly wrote 'Help!' with some assistance from McCartney. He later complained that the recording was too fast and commercialised, masking the anguish of the lyric. Nevertheless, the execution, with the backing vocals anticipating the start of each line, is thrilling.

THE NIGHT BEFORE

(Lennon-McCartney)

Although played and sung with typical conviction, this is formulaic, particularly when placed between two more innovative songs.

YOU'VE GOT TO HIDE YOUR LOVE AWAY

(Lennon-McCartney)

The most obviously Dylan-influenced Lennon song to date sees John's writing moving on to another level.

I NEED YOU

(Harrison)

Written by George for girlfriend Patti Boyd, the song's plaintive guitar riff was achieved by use of an effects pedal.

ANOTHER GIRL

(Lennon-McCartney)

The lyric might allude to difficulties in McCartney's relationship with Jane Asher, but that is the only point of interest in an otherwise routine song.

YOU'RE GOING TO LOSE THAT GIRL

(Lennon-McCartney)

The Beatles are seen 'recording' this unremarkable composition in the film.

TICKET TO RIDE

(Lennon-McCartney)

Supposedly, the title doubles as a pun on the Isle of Wight town Ryde, which, if true, neatly anglicises the Americanism. The band's heaviest moment so far, both lyrically and musically, was used to accompany the visual slapstick of Help!'s skiing sequence.

ACT NATURALLY

(Russell-Harrison)

An inspired choice for the album's Ringo moment, this version of Buck Owens' country and western ditty plays on his acting prowess and ordinary-man charm.

IT'S ONLY LOVE

(Lennon-McCartney)

Lennon later professed to despise this, and his sarcastic rolling 'r' on the word 'bright' suggests that he wasn't taking the song too seriously at the time. Nevertheless, the chorus is vigorous, and George's guitar is fed through a Leslie cabinet to resemble a Hammond organ.

YOU LIKE ME TOO MUCH

(Harrison)

An upbeat but undistinguished song composed and sung by George Harrison.

TELL ME WHAT YOU SEE

(Lennon-McCartney)

Recorded for possible inclusion in the movie but rejected by Lester, this is another throwaway effort.

I'VE JUST SEEN A FACE
(Lennon-McCartney)

Words and guitar chords tumble over each other in a breathless McCartney performance. The song was a surprise addition to wings 1976 tour set list, along with the following track.

YESTERDAY
(Lennon-McCartney)

It's easy to forget that the most covered song ever was a radical departure for the Beatles at the time, featuring McCartney alone back by a string quartet. For that reason, 'Yesterday' was never a serious contender for a UK single (it eventually came out on 7-inch vinyl in 1976). Famously, the melody came to McCartney in a dream but the lyrics caused him more difficulty. The song laboured under the working title 'Scrambled Eggs' until Paul settled on the familiar words which are often interpreted as subconsciously referring to his mother's death in 1956 when he was 14.

DIZZY MISS LIZZY
(Williams)

Bashed out at a request of US label Capitol who urgently needed some new product, this strident version of the Larry Williams song aims for but fails to achieve the same high-energy finish as 'Twist and Shout' and 'Money'.

RUBBER SOUL

Until now, the Beatles had generally produced what they described as 'work songs', although these were professionally crafted and delivered with verve. It was the influence of Bob Dylan that showed them, Lennon in particular, that pop music could be a vehicle for self-expression and that weightier topics than variations on boy meets girl could be tackled. While 'Rubber Soul' starts to move into more complex lyrical areas, the album is not a complete break with the past, rather a stepping stone towards the experimentation that would characterise 'Revolver' and 'Sgt Pepper', with new sounds being explored on almost every track. All of this puts 'Rubber Soul' into the unwelcome category of 'transitional album', but does not detract from its merits as a fine album containing the usual helping of Beatles standards.

With its distorted photo, the sleeve hints at the band's expanding consciousness, while the awful pun of the title mirrors the playfulness of some of the lyrics. In the latest of a series of breaks with tradition, the band's name does not appear on the front – by this point, the four faces alone were enough.

Acting quickly to erase the memory of the lacklustre 'Help!' and to fulfil EMI's need for product for Christmas, recording began in earnest during October 1965 and was completed in just four weeks. The sessions also produced the double A-side single 'We Can Work It Out'/'Day Tripper' songs, which would not have been out of place on 'Rubber Soul'.

Rapidly becoming more sophisticated, the Beatles had already begun to use recording technology to enhance their music but 'Rubber Soul' marks the point where they, along with producer George Martin, consciously started to use the studio as a tool.

DRIVE MY CAR
(Lennon-McCartney)

The agenda for 'Rubber Soul' is boldly announced on this tongue-in-cheek role reversal song. The 'beep beep, yeah!' chant was later adopted by Radio One as a traffic jingle.

NORWEGIAN WOOD (THIS BIRD HAS FLOWN)
(Lennon-McCartney)

The first Beatles song to feature sitar, painstakingly plucked by Harrison, this was an attempt by John to write about an affair without his wife realising. The pay-off, involving arson, is vintage Lennon.

YOU WON'T SEE ME
(Lennon-McCartney)

This stately song sees a wounded Paul pleading with Jane Asher amid some wonderful backing vocals.

NOWHERE MAN
(Lennon-McCartney)

A self-portrait of John in his 'fat Elvis' period drifting listlessly through life in his mansion in the stockbroker belt in Weybridge, Surrey. Impeccable harmonies seal a terrific ensemble performance.

THINK FOR YOURSELF
(Harrison)

Abetted by the snarling fuzz-tone bass, Harrison's song delivers a characteristic put-down.

THE WORD
(Lennon-McCartney)

The hippy philosophy is anticipated here in the first Beatles song to consciously contain a message.

MICHELLE
(Lennon-McCartney)

The song with the French chorus provided a Number 1 hit for the Overlanders in 1966. The Beatles' version falls just on the right side of kitsch.

WHAT GOES ON
(Lennon-McCartney-Starkey)

A unique three-way songwriting credit for Ringo's vocal track, a mordant country and western piece adapted from an early Lennon original.

GIRL
(Lennon-McCartney)

John's Germanic two-step was a riposte to 'Michelle' and featured 31 theatrical intakes of breath at the chorus and playful backing vocals of 'tit, tit, tit'.

I'M LOOKING THROUGH YOU
(Lennon-McCartney)

Another McCartney reflection on his relationship with Jane Asher, one in which he adopts an accusatory tone.

IN MY LIFE
(Lennon-McCartney)

Initially comprising a list of Liverpool places, Lennon eventually settled on the familiar poignant lyric with some help from McCartney. George Martin plays the electric piano solo, speeded up to achieve the 'Elizabethan' effect.

WAIT
(Lennon-McCartney)

First attempted at the 'Help!' sessions, 'Wait' was revived when the band needed another song to complete the album.

IF I NEEDED SOMEONE
(Harrison)

George's intricate melody demonstrated his increasing prowess as a songwriter. This was confirmed by a hit cover version by the Hollies, which he disliked.

RUN FOR YOUR LIFE
(Lennon-McCartney)

Detested by Lennon because it was 'knocked off' to fill the quota for 'Rubber Soul', the song borrows its opening line from Presley's 'Baby Let's Play House' and displays John's misogynistic streak. A disappointing closer to a groundbreaking album.

REVOLVER

With screaming audiences drowning out the primitive PA systems, the Beatles had atrophied as performers; live sets were reduced to barely half an hour. Their 1966 tours were marred by controversy: an inadvertent snub to first lady Imelda Marcos in Manila sparked a dangerously hostile reaction from the locals, while Lennon's remarks about the Beatles being 'bigger than Jesus' caused a furore in America, where, remarkable as it now seems, there were empty seats in many venues.

These fiascos were sufficient to persuade even McCartney, the Beatle most enamoured of live performance, that the touring had to stop, although the decision was never formally announced. The ever-increasing complexity of the music made it virtually impossible to reproduce live, meaning that the Beatles' stage act was based around old material and was no longer representative of their muse.

'Revolver' was their last album to be recorded under time pressure, before they were afforded the luxury of almost limitless hours in the studio. As such, it benefits from the expediency that urgency brings and remains their most consistently inventive collection. Its reputation has grown over the years to the point where it has been known to outperform 'Sgt Pepper' in greatest album polls.

Their status as national icons notwithstanding, the Beatles' transition from teen idols to serious artists was, in fact, accompanied by falling album sales. 'Revolver' spent a mere seven weeks at Number 1, initially selling in the region of half a million copies, 250,000 less than 'Rubber Soul'.

This trend would be spectacularly reversed with their next offering. Fellow artists, however, clearly approved, mining the album for covers, but only Cliff Bennett and the Rebel Rousers' version of 'Got To Get You Into My Life' made any impact.

TAXMAN
(Harrison)

Beginning with a muffled count-in, George's sardonic opener attacks the British Government's taxation policy for higher earners. McCartney contributes not only the distinctive bass but the guitar solo too.

ELEANOR RIGBY
(Lennon-McCartney)

Both Lennon and McCartney later claimed to have written the bulk of the lyrics of this striking voice-plus-strings track. The reality would seem to be that Lennon helped McCartney finish the song.

I'M ONLY SLEEPING
(Lennon-McCartney)

John was taking LSD almost constantly during 1966 and the wonderfully somnambulant 'I'm Only Sleeping' gives us some clue as to his state of mind at the time.

LOVE YOU TO
(Harrison)

The single sitar on 'Norwegian Wood' was hardly sufficient to prepare the audience for the full Indian treatment on George's sprightly song.

HERE, THERE AND EVERYWHERE
(Lennon-McCartney)

Exquisite three-part harmonies from Lennon, McCartney and Harrison distract the attention from Paul's sentimental lyric.

YELLOW SUBMARINE
(Lennon-McCartney)

Who else but the Beatles could get away with recording a children's song and releasing it as a single? Adults can marvel at the nautical sound effects and join in on the chorus.

SHE SAID, SHE SAID
(Lennon-McCartney)

A song based on an LSD trip of Lennon's in LA when he was with the Byrds' Roger McGuinn and David Crosby. Actor Peter Fonda provided an unwelcome interruption with his story of a near-death experience. Relief is found is the yearning 'When I was a boy' breaks.

GOOD DAY SUNSHINE
(Lennon-McCartney)

Written and recorded in the glorious summer of 1966, this is Paul at his most genial.

AND YOUR BIRD CAN SING
(Lennon-McCartney)

Lennon asserts his independence against an un-named rival, rumoured to be Mick Jagger (whose 'bird' at the time, Marianne Faithfull, could indeed sing).

FOR NO ONE
(Lennon-McCartney)

A curiously detached tale of lost love is decorated by the French horn solo, played by distinguished British musician Alan Civil.

DOCTOR ROBERT
(Lennon-McCartney)

A physician who freely administered amphetamine shots to his patients inspired this key-shifting song.

I WANT TO TELL YOU
(Harrison)

Accepted wisdom states that George Harrison matured as a songwriter towards the end of the Beatles' career, but his unprecedented three contributions to 'Revolver' would suggest that he was capable of matching Lennon and McCartney much earlier. Dominated by urgent piano, played by McCartney, 'I Want To Tell You' has a Hindu-influenced lyric.

GOT TO GET YOU INTO MY LIFE
(Lennon-McCartney)

Many years later, Paul admitted that the subject of this soul-flavoured song was in fact marijuana and not, as might have been expected, a girl.

TOMORROW NEVER KNOWS
(Lennon-McCartney)

Ringo's malapropism was used as the title for the Beatles' most experimental work yet, and his drums provide the rhythmic foundation for an astonishing collage of sound effects and tape loops. The lyrics were taken from the Tibetan Book Of The Dead, and John was famously disappointed that George Martin failed to make his voice sound like a monk chanting on a hilltop.

> "All the world is birthday cake, so take a piece, but not too much."
>
> George Harrison

SGT PEPPER'S LONELY HEARTS CLUB BAND

Probably the most discussed album ever, 'Sgt Pepper' emphatically reasserted the Beatles' cultural and commercial supremacy. Previously, Capitol had wrung ten American LPs out of the Beatles' first six British releases, but 'Pepper' was the first Beatles album with the same track listing for both markets, unleashed on the 1st of June 1967. With the Summer of Love about to reach its height, the release of 'Pepper' has been described as no less than the moment when the fractured collective consciousness of the Western World was briefly reunited.

The making of the album saw the balance of power shift away from Lennon, who had dominated the Beatles' early output, and onto McCartney, who, even before the untimely death of manager Brian Epstein, drove the project. John's assertiveness was temporarily blunted by his prodigious intake of LSD and his songwriting betrays a lack of inspiration, turning frequently to objects around him for inspiration and away from the introspection of some of his best work.

Dreaming up the title on a transatlantic flight, inspired by the vogue for long names among American West Coast groups, McCartney used it as an assumed identity for the band, a device designed to free them from being Beatles and unlock their creativity. The name also spawned the notoriously vague concept of an imaginary performance by the eponymous entertainers.

Nine months in the making, 'Pepper' was eagerly anticipated and did not disappoint. Every detail would be pored over for years to come, particularly the lavish sleeve, replete with a sheet of cardboard cut-outs. Initial copies came with a, now rare, inner bag designed by Anglo-Dutch troupe the Fool. 'Pepper' boasted another innovation – the lyrics were printed on the back cover. The album spent 27 weeks at Number 1.

SGT PEPPER'S LONELY HEARTS CLUB BAND
(Lennon-McCartney)

Crowd noises and the tuning of instruments create the illusion of live performance as a prelude to an intriguing combination of hard rock and brass band styles, complete with McCartney's huckster vocals.

WITH A LITTLE HELP FROM MY FRIENDS
(Lennon-McCartney)

Segueing from the previous track, which concluded by introducing Ringo as singer Billy Shears, this charming call-and-response number is perfectly tailored for his persona and arguably represents the definitive vehicle for the drummer's vocal talents. The 'Sgt. Pepper' concept disappears hereafter, only returning towards the end of side two.

LUCY IN THE SKY WITH DIAMONDS
(Lennon-McCartney)

Banned by the BBC on the tenuous grounds that its initials spelt LSD, John was always adamant that the song was inspired by a painting by his four-year old son Julian. The lysergic production and surreal lyrics might tend to vindicate the BBC, but Lennon was always frank about which of his songs were drug-related and there seems no reason to disbelieve him here.

GETTING BETTER
(Lennon-McCartney)

Paul's optimistic outlook is tempered somewhat by John's contribution to the lyrics and backing vocals ('It can't get no worse').

FIXING A HOLE
(Lennon-McCartney)

Long suspected of being a reference to heroin use, the reality is more prosaic – the title refers to McCartney

repairing the roof of his house. Continuing in the same vein as 'Getting Better', the track restates Paul's unshakeable self-confidence.

SHE'S LEAVING HOME
(Lennon-McCartney)

When George Martin was unavailable, due to other commitments, to score the string accompaniment, McCartney upset the producer by impatiently recruiting future Gary Glitter musical collaborator Mike Leander. Lacking Martin's delicate touch, the lachrymose arrangement drags the generation-gap song into sentimentality.

BEING FOR THE BENEFIT OF MR KITE
(Lennon-McCartney)

Needing another song for 'Pepper', Lennon turned to an antique poster advertising a circus performance in Rochdale in 1843, lifting the lyrics wholesale from it. George Martin assembled the fairground-style backing which effortlessly allows the listener to smell the sawdust.

WITHIN YOU WITHOUT YOU
(Harrison)

George is the only Beatle present, backed by uncredited Indian musicians. The song drags a little, and Harrison adopts the preachy tone that would mar some of his solo work.

WHEN I'M SIXTY FOUR
(Lennon-McCartney)

Back down to earth for an old McCartney number, revived for his father's impending birthday. The audible snigger in Paul's voice signifies that this soon-to-be middle-of-the-road standard shouldn't be taken too seriously.

LOVELY RITA
(Lennon-McCartney)

Intrigued by the American term 'meter maid', Paul constructed this light-hearted tribute to traffic wardens, which comes as something of a relief after the previous two tracks.

GOOD MORNING, GOOD MORNING
(Lennon-McCartney)

Lack of inspiration has rarely sounded so entertaining as Lennon sneers at middleclass England, drawing on Meet The Wife, a now long-forgotten BBC sitcom, and an advert for Kellogg's Corn Flakes. The track is punctuated by a punchy brass section and closes with animal noises.

SGT PEPPER'S LONELY HEARTS CLUB BAND (REPRISE)
(Lennon-McCartney)

A clucking chicken morphs into a guitar as the 'Sgt Pepper' concept makes a brief but punchy return before the encore.

A DAY IN THE LIFE
(Lennon-McCartney)

A Lennon song with some holes fixed by McCartney, this is generally regarded as the Beatles' crowning achievement. The theme is emptiness, specifically that of John's life, enlivened only by turning on to LSD. The BBC refused to play this, too, perhaps with some justification. Lennon's voice floats over the sparse backing anchored by Ringo's clattering drums, before McCartney's middle section drops in from a different song. The two orchestral crescendos were overdubbed to fill some blank bars and have often been interpreted as approximating the rush associated with certain drugs. The final ominous piano chord was created by five pairs of hands on three pianos and multi-tracked.

'Pepper' wasn't quite over – there was a snatch of backward studio gibberish (rumoured to contain a rude message) and, supposedly, a noise at a frequency only audible to dogs.

MAGICAL MYSTERY TOUR

After four years of enjoying almost untouchable status, the Beatles finally fell from grace when their colourful 50-minute television special Magical Mystery Tour was first screened, in black and white, on BBC 1 on Boxing Day 1967. Largely plot-free, the movie puzzled and enraged viewers expecting loveable moptop antics and was savaged by the critics. Viewed from a modern perspective, Magical Mystery Tour is a quaint period piece, the undoubted high point of which is the amazing performance of 'I Am The Walrus'.

Although Capitol have been criticised for milking the Beatles' catalogue dry, the American arm of EMI actually came up with a better package here in the form of an album featuring the six songs from the film on side one with recent non-album cuts on the reverse. In Britain, the new material came in an unusual double EP and booklet combination. The Extended Play format was familiar to Beatles fans – Parlophone had issued 11 Beatles EPs between 1963 and 1966, only one of which, 'Long Tall Sally', contained new material, proving that the British label was equally adept at exploitation.

The Capitol LP was freely available on import until its belated release in November 1976 and has become the only non-UK album accepted as part of the official canon. Before the rash of Beatles compilations in the Seventies, it was the best place to find their greatest 7-inch, 'Penny Lane/Strawberry Fields Forever', which was severed from 'Sgt Pepper' when Parlophone demanded a new single early in 1967. The double A-side highlighted more than ever before the very different muses of Lennon and McCartney, while, paradoxically, the two songs seem inextricably bound together.

MAGICAL MYSTERY TOUR
(Lennon-McCartney)

Fulfilling the same role as the title track of 'Sgt Pepper', this suffers by comparison, although it is a pleasing enough combination of brass, harmonies and effects.

THE FOOL ON THE HILL
(Lennon-McCartney)

This McCartney ode to an idiot savant is one of the musical highlights of the Magical Mystery Tour venture.

FLYING
(Lennon-McCartney-Harrison-Starkey)

The only instrumental released by the Beatles during the band's lifetime and the first piece credited to all four members.

BLUE JAY WAY
(Harrison)

Despite an atmospheric opening, George's tale of waiting for friends who are lost in LA fails to go anywhere

YOUR MOTHER SHOULD KNOW
(Lennon-McCartney)

A typically catchy McCartney melody is thrown away on an inconsequential song.

I AM THE WALRUS
(Lennon-McCartney)

The Beatles' final excursion into psychedelia, although the term hardly does justice to this dense amalgam of sound. Based around the old two-note police siren, the song features one of John's most impenetrable lyrics, which was designed to confound teachers and pupils at his old school after he discovered that they had been analysing Beatles songs.

HELLO GOODBYE

(Lennon-McCartney)

Anyone searching for a similar message to 'All You Need Is Love' from its follow-up would have been disappointed, but Paul's lightweight confection of contradictory statements was impossibly infectious. The closing chant was used over the end titles of the film.

STRAWBERRY FIELDS FOREVER

(Lennon-McCartney)

Two separate versions were patched together by George Martin, and although the edit is apparent, it merely adds to the mystique of Lennon's masterpiece. The stumbling lyric sees him searching for identity with Strawberry Field (without the 's'), a childhood haunt representing the certainty he knew as a boy.

PENNY LANE

(Lennon-McCartney)

Paul's Liverpool song is actually redolent of Swinging London in its confident swagger. The cheeky lyric incorporates both a rude Scouse joke ('finger pie') and surrealism ('she feels as if she's in a play'). 'Penny Lane' is McCartney at the height of his powers.

BABY YOU'RE A RICH MAN

(Lennon-McCartney)

The B-side of 'All You Need Is Love' is something of a stoned doodle with verses by Lennon and the chorus by McCartney.

ALL YOU NEED IS LOVE

(Lennon-McCartney)

Despite bans for alleged drug references and the inexplicable failure of 'Penny Lane'/'Strawberry Fields Forever' to reach Number 1, the Beatles were still the only choice for Britain's contribution to the pioneering global TV satellite link-up Our World, screened on the 25th of June 1967. Lennon wrote the simple, anthemic 'All You Need Is Love' especially for the show. It is now virtually impossible to hear the Marseillaise, France's national anthem, without bursting into a chorus of 'love, love, love'.

> "I'm not going to change the way I look or the way I feel to conform to anything. I've always been a freak. So I've been a freak all my life and I have to live with that, you know. I'm one of those people."
>
> John Lennon

THE BEATLES

Universally known as the 'White Album' after its minimalist sleeve, this mammoth 30-track double set was a conscious reaction to 'Sgt Pepper' by the Beatles, both in content and artwork. The sessions were legendarily fractious, with the normally placid Ringo storming out after an argument with McCartney, while Yoko Ono's constant presence by John's side aggravated his bandmates. With individual Beatles often working separately in different studios (and corridors) at Abbey Road, there is inevitably less of an ensemble feel about the album with the group operating as two, sometimes three, different entities.

A favourite pastime among fans and critics alike is to edit the 'White Album' down to a single LP, with many believing that, like most double albums, it would have benefited from some judicious pruning; producer George Martin was also of that opinion. The sheer scope of its 30 tracks allows the Beatles some indulgences that might have otherwise have been left for the bootleggers to pick over. The alternative argument holds that the 'White Album's' strength lies in its diversity.

Having spent some time in early 1968 learning transcendental meditation in India at the Rishikesh headquarters of the Maharishi Mahesh Yogi at the foothills of the Himalayas, Lennon, McCartney and Harrison returned with a stash of new songs that comprised the majority of the album.

The album is darker in tone than 'Sgt Pepper', reflecting the turbulent world of 1968. Charles Manson used some songs, 'Helter Skelter' and 'Piggies' in particular, to justify the appalling murders committed by his 'family' in Los Angeles the following year.

BACK IN THE USSR
(Lennon-McCartney)

In the absence of Ringo, Paul occupied the drum stool for this marvellous piece of lampoonery, which, somewhat controversially during the Cold War, relocated the stylistic trappings of Chuck Berry and the Beach Boys to the Soviet Union.

DEAR PRUDENCE
(Lennon-McCartney)

The first song to feature the fingerpicking guitar style learnt from Donovan in India was written by Lennon to entice Prudence Farrow, Mia's sister, out of her chalet.

GLASS ONION
(Lennon-McCartney)

John mischievously misdirects those who scoured the Beatles' records for enlightenment. His most misleading 'clue', that 'the Walrus was Paul', was intended as a tribute to McCartney's efforts to keep the band together.

OB-LA-DI, OB-LA-DA
(Lennon-McCartney)

Conga player Jimmy Scott, who appears on the track, was fond of using the title phrase, which means 'life goes on' in Yoruba dialect. McCartney constructed a reggae song peopled with Jamaican characters around it, although Scott was actually Nigerian. Its release as a single was vetoed by Lennon, who disliked it, so Marmalade had the hit.

WILD HONEY PIE
(Lennon-McCartney)

A discordant McCartney solo fragment that segues into the following song.

THE CONTINUING STORY OF BUNGALOW BILL
(Lennon-McCartney)

Another song written by John in India, this pokes fun at one Richard Cooke III, who, while visiting his mother at Rishikesh, participated in a tiger hunt. Yoko Ono pops up to sing one line.

WHILE MY GUITAR GENTLY WEEPS
(Harrison)

Eric Clapton became the first high-profile, if uncredited, guest to appear on a Beatles track when asked by his friend George Harrison to play guitar (George repaid the favour on Cream's 'Badge'). Harrison's ulterior motive was to put the Beatles on their best behaviour in the presence of an outsider. The result is somewhat overcooked.

HAPPINESS IS A WARM GUN
(Lennon-McCartney)

A typically unconventional Lennon piece, which incorporates a surreal, free-associative lyric, four-part structure and idiosyncratic time signatures, plus the obligatory nod to Yoko ('Mother Superior').

MARTHA MY DEAR
(Lennon-McCartney)

The knowledge that this is a love song to his Old English sheepdog, does not detract from a mellifluous McCartney creation.

I'M SO TIRED
(Lennon-McCartney)

Alternating between lethargy and anger, John includes one of his most amusing lines, attacking the man who brought tobacco to England.

BLACKBIRD
(Lennon-McCartney)

Sometimes interpreted as supporting the black civil rights movement in America, it seems more likely that this gentle McCartney solo turn was written about a blackbird singing outside his window in India.

PIGGIES
(Harrison)

In stark contrast to his peaceful spiritual views, Harrison viciously condemns straight society on 'Piggies'.

ROCKY RACCOON
(Lennon-McCartney)

Paul's whimsical piece about comical cowboys falls flat in the absence of a punchline.

DON'T PASS ME BY
(Starkey)

Ringo was finally pushed by his colleagues into completing a song he'd been working on for five years, if references in interviews are anything to go by. Country-tinged, as you might expect, the song is unremarkable and a little overlong.

WHY DON'T WE DO IT IN THE ROAD?
(Lennon-McCartney)

Recorded by McCartney in a corridor in Abbey Road while the others were working elsewhere, Ringo overdubbed his drums later. The song was inspired by watching monkeys copulate in India and consists of Paul hollering minimal lyrics to a hard-rock backing.

I WILL
(Lennon-McCartney)

With brilliant sequencing, the contrasting side of McCartney's talents is showcased on this plaintive acoustic number.

JULIA
(Lennon-McCartney)

Lennon's own acoustic piece ended the first record. The lyrics are fraught with significance; the title refers to his late mother, while 'Yoko' means 'Ocean child' in Japanese.

BIRTHDAY
(Lennon-McCartney)

Birthday songs are both sent up and celebrated, with the Beatles at their most raucous.

YER BLUES
(Lennon-McCartney)

John's pain is very real but leavened by some tragicomic exaggerations (and the matter-of-fact title). He clearly rated the song highly, performing it on the Rolling Stones Rock And Roll Circus, a TV special that remained unseen for many years, and with the Plastic Ono Band on 'Live Peace in Toronto'.

MOTHER NATURE'S SON
(Lennon-McCartney)

Another solo turn from Paul, accompanied only by unknown brass players on a song that suggests that their sojourn in India had its idyllic moments.

EVERYBODY'S GOT SOMETHING TO HIDE EXCEPT ME AND MY MONKEY
(Lennon-McCartney)

The frantic pace distracts from the fact that Lennon appears to have little to say other than contradictory statements reminiscent of 'Hello Goodbye'. 'My Monkey' is a rather unflattering reference to Yoko.

SEXY SADIE
(Lennon-McCartney)

After leaving the camp in Rishikesh disillusioned with what he perceived as the Maharishi's more worldly appetites, Lennon penned a scathing attack on him but changed the lyrics to avoid legal repercussions.

HELTER SKELTER
(Lennon-McCartney)

Reading a misleading report in the music press that the Who had recorded the loudest rock track ever (actually 'I Can See For Miles'), the ever-competitive McCartney decided that the Beatles should go one better. Unusually, he forgot to include a tune.

LONG, LONG, LONG
(Harrison)

An underrated acoustic Harrison piece, which, at first glance, appears to be a love song but is, in fact, concerned with his devotion to the divine.

REVOLUTION 1
(Lennon-McCartney)

The first version of the song, which, in its definitive form, featured on the B-side of 'Hey Jude', is slower and features Lennon vacillating between being counted in or out of the revolution. The re-recorded version resolves the issue with a firm 'count me out'.

HONEY PIE
(Lennon-McCartney)

Paul's pastiche of Thirties stylings is immaculate but somehow empty.

SAVOY TRUFFLE
(Harrison)

George had better songs than this, which he began to stockpile and used on his solo debut, 'All Things Must Pass'. Concerned with one of Eric Clapton's lesser-known addictions, chocolate, it doubles as a comment on the greed of consumer society.

CRY BABY CRY
(Lennon-McCartney)

Several of John's 'White Album' songs have a child-like ambience and here, on one of his less celebrated pieces, the atmosphere is one of understated creepiness.

REVOLUTION 9
(Lennon-McCartney)

The most controversial and subversive track ever to bear the Beatles' name. McCartney's ghostly 'take me back' song fragment sets the mood for a sinister sound collage designed to provide an aural impression of revolution. Assembled by Lennon with some help from Harrison; Paul, who regarded himself as the avant-garde Beatle, was in New York when it was recorded.

GOOD NIGHT
(Lennon-McCartney)

Generally assumed to be a McCartney vehicle for Ringo, the lushly orchestrated 'Good Night' was, in fact, the work of Lennon, written for son Julian.

YELLOW SUBMARINE

The Beatles largely distanced themselves from the animated film, which was made in the UK but instigated by King Features, producers of the American Beatles cartoon series. Contractually obliged to furnish the filmmakers with four new songs, the band supplied a combination of rejects and knock-offs. Originally intended for release as an EP, the idea was dropped because the format was obsolete in America. The material was padded out to album length by the addition of the title song and 'All You Need Is Love', which played a pivotal role in the film's climax, plus extracts from George Martin's soundtrack, similar to the US soundtrack albums of the first two films. A 'Songtrack' version featuring all the songs from the movie, in remixed form, was released in 1997.

ONLY A NORTHERN SONG
(Harrison)

A 'Sgt Pepper' out-take recorded as a joke, according to its composer George Harrison, to fulfil his obligations to Northern Songs, Lennon/McCartney's publishing company.

ALL TOGETHER NOW
(Lennon-McCartney)

Childish, repetitive McCartney song, which speeds mercifully to a close.

HEY BULLDOG
(Lennon-McCartney)

The best of the four new songs, 'Hey Bulldog' was recorded when the band convened to film a promo for 'Lady Madonna', quickly becoming the contract filler for Yellow Submarine. Featuring a menacing piano intro and coruscating guitar solo, the track falls short of greatness due to its silly, improvised ending.

IT'S ALL TOO MUCH
(Harrison)
Already dated when the album was released in January
1969, this overlong psychedelic effort was recorded some
18 months earlier.

PEPPERLAND/ SEA OF TIME/SEA OF HOLES/
SEA OF MONSTERS/ MARCH OF THE MEANIES/
PEPPERLAND LAID WASTE/ YELLOW SUBMARINE
IN PEPPERLAND
Side two of the album was taken up by George Martin's
orchestral score from the film. Only the closing track is
based directly on a Beatles song, 'Yellow Submarine'.

> "First and foremost
> I am a drummer.
> After that, I'm other
> things... But I didn't
> play drums to make
> money."
>
> Ringo Starr

ABBEY ROAD

After spending a miserable month in January 1969 on the ill-fated 'Get Back' project – which, as 'Let It Be', would be the last Beatles album released – there was barely a pause before they started work on what would become the final album they recorded. The sessions lasted until August, when the Beatles assembled in the studio for the final time for the sequencing of 'Abbey Road'. Paul had invited George Martin back to produce them; consequently, 'Abbey Road' regains the polished sheen of 'Sgt Pepper' and was Martin's favourite Beatles album.

The bulk of side two of the original vinyl was taken up by the 'Long Medley', a unique series of snippets and fragments woven together to create the impression of unity, although several of the individual pieces refer to and were recorded in the knowledge that this was the Beatles' last stand. The medley's main architect was McCartney; Lennon at first expressed enthusiasm for the idea but quickly changed his mind and disowned it. Although the sessions were less ill-tempered than those for the 'White Album' or 'Let It Be', the unified front is something of an illusion, with the composer of each song generally taking the lead. The iconic sleeve helped fuel the bizarre 'Paul is dead' rumours that swept America in October 1969.

COME TOGETHER
(Lennon-McCartney)

This started life as a song for LSD guru Timothy Leary's short-lived campaign to run for governor of California. Using Chuck Berry's 'You Can't Catch Me' as its basis (and leaving in the first line, for which Lennon was later sued), John's swamp-rocker boasts a quasi-nonsensical, vaguely unpleasant lyric.

SOMETHING
(Harrison)

George's best-known and most covered song finally afforded him equal status to Lennon and McCartney. As the first Beatles single lifted from an already-released album, it became George's only British A-side.

MAXWELL'S SILVER HAMMER
(Lennon-McCartney)

An unfairly maligned McCartney piece, this is the story of a serial killer set to cheery music, achieving a mildly unsettling effect.

OH! DARLING
(Lennon-McCartney)

John expressed the view that his voice would have been better suited to this doo-wop pastiche, but Paul exercised composer's rights, reviving his Little Richard voice to perform the song.

OCTOPUS'S GARDEN
(Starkey)

Ringo's second solo composition returns him to the aquatic environment of 'Yellow Submarine'.

I WANT YOU (SHE'S SO HEAVY)
(Lennon-McCartney)

Rivalling 'Helter Skelter' as the Beatles heaviest moment, 'I Want You' is a two-piece song built around an insistent, descending riff, the lyrics of which consist almost entirely of the title. It ends abruptly.

HERE COMES THE SUN
(Harrison)

George's simple, optimistic piece was written in Eric Clapton's garden using the arrival of the sun as a metaphor for the relief of a break from the Beatles' business meetings.

BECAUSE

(Lennon-McCartney)

Based on Beethoven's 'Moonlight Sonata', 'Because' features three-part harmonies and continues the mellow mood at the start of side two.

YOU NEVER GIVE ME YOUR MONEY

(Lennon-McCartney)

'The Long Medley' begins with a piece in three parts: the first a sorrowful meditation on the Beatles' business wranglings, then a fantasy of escape, and finally, the hope of salvation via an old children's song.

SUN KING

(Lennon-McCartney)

A beatific piece that demonstrates that Lennon was equally fluent in gibberish in Italian, Spanish and Portuguese as in his native tongue.

MEAN MR. MUSTARD

(Lennon-McCartney)

John's scabrous vignette about a miser was inspired by a newspaper article, like many of his songs.

POLYTHENE PAM

(Lennon-McCartney)

A character based on an amalgam of two women from the Beatles' past – a fan who had the habit of eating polythene and the girlfriend of beat poet Royston Ellis, filtered through Lennon's fertile imagination.

SHE CAME IN THROUGH THE BATHROOM WINDOW

(Lennon-McCartney)

One of the fans, known as Apple Scruffs, who camped outside Abbey Road and McCartney's nearby St. John's Wood residence, broke into the house, providing Paul with the starting point for this piece.

GOLDEN SLUMBERS

(Lennon-McCartney)

The old English lullaby is set to new music by McCartney and given additional lyrics, which allude to the dissolution of the band, a theme developed in the following tracks.

CARRY THAT WEIGHT

(Lennon-McCartney)

McCartney rightly predicts that the Beatles will cast a long shadow over their own lives; to underline the point, the crucial line is sung by all four Beatles.

THE END

(Lennon-McCartney)

'You Never Give Me Your Money' is reprised before alternating guitar solos from McCartney, Harrison and Lennon (in that order). Paul's simple, karmic statement then brings the Beatles' recording career to an end – but not quite.

HER MAJESTY

(Lennon-McCartney)

Edited from between 'Mean Mr Mustard' and 'Polythene Pam', hence the jagged opening, 'Her Majesty' was discovered by Paul at the end of a tape after 20 seconds of silence. Liking the pomposity-puncturing effect, he left in his tongue-in-cheek tribute to the Queen.

LET IT BE

McCartney was the Beatle who most missed live performance, and the origins of 'Let It Be' lay in his attempts to persuade his colleagues that a return to the concert arena would reunite and refocus the squabbling band.

Locations as diverse as London's Roundhouse, Liverpool Cathedral and a Roman amphitheatre in Tunisia were mooted, before the intractability of the other three Beatles scuppered the project. The proposed documentary of the Beatles rehearsing for the show would have served as promotion for the gig. In the event, the film provided United Artists with their long overdue third Beatle movie, finally released in May 1970.

What the cameras saw in January 1969 were some lacklustre rehearsals at Twickenham Film Studios, during which the tensions that dogged the sessions for the 'White Album' resurfaced. This time, George Harrison walked out. Relocating to the more conducive environment of the newly completed Apple Studio in Savile Row was not enough to prevent the Beatles from abandoning it, with countless hours of unfinished material in the can.

Although engineer Glyn Johns compiled two versions of the album in 1969, the band could not agree, and, eventually, Lennon brought in legendary American producer Phil Spector to assemble the finished release. Spector, famous for his 'wall of sound' technique, was an odd choice for the Beatles' back-to-basics project, and Paul was less than happy with the results. Even the snatches of studio chat between songs proved controversial, with Lennon seeming to mock McCartney's numbers, particularly the childishly voiced intro to the title track. The album 'as it was meant to be' without Spector's input, was finally released in 2003 as 'Let It Be Naked'.

TWO OF US
(Lennon-McCartney)

It is likely that John believed 'Two Of Us' was about himself and McCartney as teenagers, but, in fact, it was written about Paul and Linda, who liked to take long drives in the country, getting lost in the process. The song captures a freewheeling, bohemian spirit.

DIG A PONY
(Lennon-McCartney)

Lennon made up the verses on the spot, while the chorus comes from a different piece.

ACROSS THE UNIVERSE
(Lennon-McCartney)

Recorded in February 1968, 'Across the Universe' was passed over as a single in favour of 'Lady Madonna' and subsequently donated to World Wildlife Fund charity album 'No One's Gonna Change Our World', a venture led by Spike Milligan. Phil Spector finished it by adding strings and choirs.

I ME MINE
(Harrison)

Set to waltz time, George's sour reflection on greed and selfishness was the last track the Beatles worked on (minus Lennon, who was out of the country) in April 1970, when a properly recorded version of the song, seen being rehearsed in the film, was required.

DIG IT
(Lennon-McCartney-Harrison-Starkey)

A short studio improvisation, credited to all four Beatles, mainly consisting of Lennon reeling off a list of names and the title phrase.

LET IT BE
(Lennon-McCartney)

The final Beatles single came in a slightly different version on the album. Although it conveniently appeared to the band's epitaph, the song had been recorded in January 1969. Its hymn-like atmosphere was reinforced by references to 'mother Mary' which Paul, in fact, intended as a tribute to his late mother.

MAGGIE MAE
(Trad, arr: Lennon-McCartney-Harrison-Starkey)

A snatch of the ribald Liverpool folk song often used by the band as a warm-up number was the last non-original track to be released by the Beatles.

I'VE GOT A FEELING
(Lennon-McCartney)

Two separate songs are brought together, adding Lennon's 'Everybody Had A Hard Year' to McCartney's 'I've Got A Feeling'. The loose feel successfully brings off the combination.

ONE AFTER 909
(Lennon-McCartney)

The Beatles warmed up during the 'Let It Be' sessions by playing many old rock'n'roll favourites, none of which made the final cut. A very early Lennon/McCartney song, 'One After 909' had been attempted in 1963 but failed to impress George Martin.

THE LONG AND WINDING ROAD
(Lennon-McCartney)

McCartney was incensed when he discovered that Spector had, without his knowledge, plastered what amounted to a demo of the song, with mushy strings and heavenly choirs. Having concealed from him the fact that Spector was working on the material, Lennon was held equally culpable. More than any other single factor, this led to Paul's announcement that he'd left the group. Beneath the controversy lies one of Paul's most beautiful songs, inspired by the terrain around his farm in Scotland. Sadly, it was never fully realised.

FOR YOU BLUE
(Harrison)

George's final contribution is something of a contradiction in terms, a 'happy-go-lucky' 12-bar blues, written for his wife Patti.

GET BACK
(Lennon-McCartney)

Evolving from an ambiguous satire on anti-immigration views, 'Get Back' had its political content removed but still embraced coy references to pot smoking and gender-bending. The single cut of Paul's bluesy rocker was released in February 1969, a year before the album, in a different version. Neither were taken from the famous rooftop performance in January 1969 although applause and chat is dubbed onto both the beginning and the end. Lennon's facetious remark, 'I hope we've passed the audition', provides an oddly apt ending.